© 2009 Van H. White

ABOUT THE AUTHOR

MARK DI VINCENZO worked as a journalist for twenty-four years, making a name for himself as a reporter who exposed abuses and as a writer who made the complicated seem simple. During that time he won numerous awards, then he became an editor. He left daily journalism in the summer of 2007 to start Business Writers Group, a company that writes for corporate clients. Born and reared in Cleveland, he lives in Newport News, a shipyard town in coastal Virginia, with his wife and two youngest daughters. His oldest daughter attends the University of Oklahoma. *Buy Ketchup in May and Fly at Noon: A Guide to the Best Time to Buy This, Do That and Go There* is his first book.

BUY KETCHUP IN MAY AND FLY AT NOON

BUY KETCHUP IN MAY AND FLY AT NOON

A Guide to the Best Time to
Buy This, Do That and Go There

MARK DI VINCENZO

HARPER

NEW YORK · LONDON · TORONTO · SYDNEY

HARPER

HarperCollins books may be purchased for educational, business, or sales promotional use. For information please write: Special Markets Department, HarperCollins Publishers, 10 East 53rd Street, New York, NY 10022.

FIRST EDITION

Designed by Justin Dodd

Library of Congress Cataloging-in-Publication Data
Di Vincenzo, Mark.
   Buy ketchup in May and fly at noon : a guide to the best time to do this, buy that and go there / Mark Di Vincenzo. — 1st ed.
      p.   cm.
   ISBN 978-0-06-173088-7
1. Consumer education. 2. Time management. I. Title.
TX335.D52   2009
640—dc22
                                                                                        2009022017

09 10 11 12 13   OV/RRD   10 9 8 7 6 5 4

FOR JAYNE

CONTENTS

ACKNOWLEDGMENTS

Thanks to everyone who provided information for this book.

Thanks to my editor, Kate Nintzel, for your precision, your enthusiasm, and your patience.

Thanks to my agent, Michelle Wolfson, for believing in this book and for doing my blocking and tackling.

Thanks to Jayne, my mighty wife, always supportive, always encouraging, always loving.

INTRODUCTION

Ilive with a wonderful woman who occasionally wakes up in the middle of the night and stumbles around our dark bedroom in search of paper and a pen and then spends the next few minutes—or hours—scribbling down the terrific ideas that popped into her head while she was trying to sleep.

This happened at about three-thirty one summer morning in 2007, and a few hours later, after I awoke, she turned off her hair dryer, picked up a legal pad, rushed over to me, and said, "You've got to listen to this!" *This* was an idea for a book I should write—about the best time to do things. After she explained it to me, she handed me her notes, and I read her early-morning scribbles and concluded that it really *was* a great idea. Then I proceeded to do absolutely nothing with it. I was writing another, very different book that excited me, so I put her book idea on the back burner. But it didn't want to settle for that position. I couldn't stop thinking about it.

People are always talking about the best time to do this or that, or buy this or that, or go here or there, and I couldn't help but think that they would want answers to the questions my wife wrote on that legal pad and others that I added to her list.

So about a month later, I wrote the first draft of a book proposal, the seed for *Buy Ketchup in May and Fly at Noon: A Guide to the Best Time to Buy This, Do That, and Go There.*

Buy Ketchup in May Fly at Noon couldn't come at a better time. A credit crisis and recession have gripped the world, stifling economies. Pay raises aren't keeping pace with cost-of-living expenses, the rising prices of everything from heating oil and gasoline to milk, eggs, and bread. The world's largest banks, tangled in bad mortgage debt, have been reduced to begging for money from their governments. Homeowners are watching and agonizing as the value of their homes drop, and many can't pay their mortgages. Retirement nest eggs are shrinking as stock markets in the United States, Europe, and Asia experience record-setting fluctuations. And if that weren't bad enough, health-care costs and health insurance continue to soar. All of this has contributed to an increasing hunger by most everyone to save money however, whenever, and wherever they can.

Enter *Buy Ketchup in May and Fly at Noon.*

The book provides dozens and dozens of money-saving tips about the best time to buy everything from shoes and Champagne to horses and houses. You'll also learn the best time to ask for a raise, hunt for a job, and go to garage sales.

But *Buy Ketchup in May and Fly at Noon* isn't just about saving you money. It's also about saving you time, making you smarter, and giving you information to help you live longer and improve your relationships.

In this book, you'll discover the best time of day to do a cardio workout, make love, eat a snack, and take a nap. The best day of the week to go to a restaurant, fire someone, and see the *Mona Lisa*. The best time of the year to go to Disney World, the Grand Canyon, and Mount Rushmore.

Buy Ketchup in May and Fly at Noon is crammed with hundreds of practical tips.

I should point out that I'm not a source for any of the information in this book. I'm a long-time journalist who never includes his opinions in the stories he writes. Same goes for this book. The answers within came from experts—people I either interviewed or whose findings I came across in books, magazines, or academic and scientific journals. To the best of my knowledge, everything in this book is accurate, but sometimes experts are wrong, and sometimes they disagree. So when it comes to serious issues, such as your health and your finances, don't replace what you read here with the advice you'll receive from your doctor, lawyer, financial adviser, and others who are licensed to help you make important decisions.

I hope you enjoy reading this book as much as I've enjoyed researching and writing it.

Let the questions and answers begin!

CHAPTER ONE

FOR SALE

There really *is* a best time to do just about anything and everything, and that's especially true when it comes to buying things. This chapter—the longest in the book— tells you the best time to buy everything from shoes, appliances, and bread to bicycles, NFL tickets, and cars, and like the rest of the book, it explains why the best times are the best times. You'll also find out the best time to shop at thrift stores, warehouse stores, and flea markets and the best time to return merchandise, negotiate a discount, and buy an extended warranty. Follow this advice and save anywhere from a few bucks to thousands of dollars.

WHEN IS THE BEST TIME OF THE DAY TO BUY SHOES? Late afternoon. That's when your feet have swelled and are at their largest size. Buying shoes in the late afternoon means they'll fit just fine in the morning when your feet are at their smallest. But more importantly, it means they'll fit after a full day of being on your feet when you need them to be most comfortable. **Shopping tip:** Your feet look like they're the same size, but chances are one is slightly larger than the other. So when you try on shoes, buy the size that fits the larger foot the best. **Did you know?** Feet can increase in size as you get older. They're not growing, but tendons and ligaments often get stretched out over time. If you haven't bought new shoes in a while, have your feet measured first.

WHEN IS THE BEST MONTH TO BUY SNEAKERS? April or November. Athletic shoe companies sponsor charity walks and races throughout the year, but many are in April, when nonserious runners start hitting the pavement again. Sales tend to accompany these races. Check for November sales at big-box retailers, which need to make room for winter boots and shoes. **Money-saving tip:** Keep an eye out for store closings. That's when you may see $120 sneakers sell for as little as $20, and it suddenly makes sense for serious runners who go through three or four pairs a year to buy ten or twelve.

WHEN IS THE BEST TIME AND DAY OF THE WEEK TO BUY CLOTHING? Thursday evenings, approximately six weeks after items arrive in stores. If clothes haven't sold about six weeks after they arrive in stores, managers start lowering the prices. These sales often occur as part of weekend sales, which usually start on Thursday. Shop after work or on your lunch hour on Thursdays; by the weekend, most everything has been picked over. **Another view:** Wednesdays. Some national chains, including Gap and Banana Republic, put clothes on sale midweek. **Best day of the year?** December 26. Department stores tend to slash prices that day. **FYI:** There are good deals to be had year round at department stores for those shopping for off-season garments.

WHEN IS THE BEST MONTH TO BUY SWIMSUITS? September. Swimsuit sales tend to start in August, but by September, department stores badly want to get rid of swimsuits and other summer items. If they don't do so by September, swimsuits often are sold at a loss to discounters, which store them in their warehouses and start selling them in May for a lot more than what you would have paid in September.

WHEN IS THE BEST MONTH TO BUY A WINTER COAT? January or February. Coats and winter clothes go on sale then. The longer you wait, the lower the prices—retailers will need to make room for spring clothing. **Keep in mind:** The longer you wait, the worse the selection will get.

WHEN IS THE BEST MONTH OF THE YEAR TO BUY JEANS? October. Wait until the post-back-to-school sales end in September, and you'll see deep discounts, especially during fall seasons when denim is not expected to be a big part of fashion trends. Lower demand quickly leads to lower prices.

WHEN IS THE BEST DAY OF THE WEEK TO SHOP AT DEPARTMENT STORES? Saturday evenings. Department store ads come out in the Sunday newspaper, and store employees usually have a lot to markdown, so they start putting up signs and changing prices on Saturday evening. **FYI:** If you're there then, some store managers will sell you what you want at sale prices. If you're not so lucky, go back Sunday morning and buy what you scouted out Saturday—at the new low price.

WHEN IS THE BEST TIME TO DO BACK-TO-SCHOOL SHOPPING? Mid- to late September. Many retailers will lure shoppers in August with incredible deals—a penny for a bottle of glue, twenty cents for box of crayons, twenty-five cents for a pack of notebook paper—which they refer to as "loss leaders" because they may lose money on them. The retailers are willing to lose money on a few items to get you in the store to buy other school supplies and back-to-school clothes at full price. Try to wait until after school starts to stock up on the back-to-school items that weren't on sale in August. Many of these items go on sale in September, when stores try to get rid of them to make room for fall merchandise. **Other money-saving tips:** 1) If you can, buy a school year's worth of supplies and clothes for your children in September, even if that means guessing the sizes they'll wear in the winter and spring. 2) If you don't have the space to store a whole year's worth of school supplies in September, be on the lookout for good deals year round. The more you can avoid buying school supplies in August, the more money you'll save.

WHEN IS THE BEST TIME TO STOCK UP AT WAREHOUSE STORES? Days before your membership expires. Stock up, and then let your membership lapse. You won't need to return to that store for another two or three months. Renew your membership then. By waiting, you'll save a few months' membership dues. **Did you know?** For many items, the average markup at warehouse stores is about half of the markup at grocery stores. But one study shows that shoppers assume all warehouse store items are cheaper, causing them to buy more of everything, ultimately spending more at warehouse stores than they would at grocery stores.

WHEN IS THE BEST TIME OF THE MONTH TO SHOP AT A THRIFT STORE? Right after the dry cleaners and clothing stores make their donations. Many thrift stores receive monthly donations from local businesses, especially dry cleaners, which give clothes that customers fail to pick up to thrift stores. At many dry cleaners, space is of critical importance, so they give away abandoned clothes once or twice a month. Get chummy with the workers

at your neighborhood thrift store and ask them when they typically receive these donations, which are brand new if they're coming from stores or are freshly laundered or dry
cleaned if they're from dry cleaners. **Related tip:** When you're shopping at a thrift store,
always look for items with dry cleaning tags on them. People who buy quality garments
often have them professionally cleaned to keep them in good condition, so you can assume those clothes are well made. And then there are those people who are so conscien-
tious that they take the clothes they plan to donate to the dry cleaners before they drop
them off at the thrift store. Either way, you win.

WHEN IS THE BEST TIME OF THE YEAR TO SHOP AT A THRIFT STORE? The spring, when homeowners start cleaning out their attics and having garage sales. Items that don't sell often
end up at thrift stores. If thrift stores get very crowded with merchandise, managers will
mark down merchandise, especially winter items. **Bottom line:** The best time to shop at a
thrift store is the off-season, when you'll find the best deals. Buy shorts, swimsuits, and
bicycles in the fall and the winter, and look for heavy coats, scarves, and gloves in the
spring and the summer.

WHEN IS THE BEST TIME OF THE YEAR TO SHOP AT A WARM-WEATHER OUTDOOR FLEA MARKET?
The spring. If you live in a colder climate where outdoor flea markets close in the winter,
make sure you find out when they reopen and show up that weekend. Sellers have been
stockpiling antiques, household items, and knickknacks all winter and want to exchange
them for some cash.

WHEN IS THE BEST TIME OF THE DAY TO GO TO A GARAGE SALE TO FIND A REAL TREASURE? Before it's
scheduled to open. That's when antique shop owners and other store owners get there,

and they know what they're looking for and how much it should cost. So educate yourself as much as possible about what you're looking to buy, and buy it before the store owners do. A small percentage of sellers won't sell you anything until the advertised opening time, but most will because they no longer want what they're selling. Why disappoint a buyer who may leave and not return?

WHEN IS THE BEST TIME OF THE DAY TO GO TO A FLEA MARKET OR GARAGE SALE TO FIND THE BEST DEAL? Right before it closes. Late in the day, sellers begin to dread packing up their stuff and storing it or taking it to a thrift store to donate. Remember, if they wanted to keep their stuff, it wouldn't be on a card table in their driveway or on a blanket on their lawn. **FYI:** Garage sales are especially good places to shop during recessions or when the economy is otherwise slumping. Sellers need extra money and are more likely to drop prices. If you've got some extra cash, it can be money well spent.

WHEN IS THE BEST TIME AND DAY TO END AN EBAY AUCTION? Between 6 p.m. and 9 p.m., Sunday. That's when people tend to have the most free time—churchgoers are home by then—and are more likely to be on their computers for leisure purposes. The most intense bidding occurs just before an auction ends, and you want to have more people online then.

WHEN IS THE BEST TIME TO BUY SOMETHING AT A LIVE AUCTION? Toward the end. This is especially true if it's an auction with hundreds of lots. People tend to bid more than they should at the beginning of an auction because their adrenaline is flowing and they're excited, and because they have more money early on, before they've bought anything else. Lucky you if you want an item scheduled to be sold toward the end. You'll compete against fewer bidders because many have spent more than they thought they would and have gone home. If you're a seller and you hired an auctioneer to sell an estate or a house full of stuff, make sure he knows to auction off the pricey items at the beginning. **What about eBay?** Same thing. Wait until just before the deadline and then bid. This buying practice is called "sniping," and researchers have found that those who do it best often get the best deals because they're not tipping off the other buyers that an item is worth more than it eventually will sell for. **FYI:** About half of all eBay auctions involve overbidding, other researchers have found. Buyers sometimes miss an opportunity to purchase an item at a fixed price from one seller and subsequently pay more for the same item from a seller who doesn't offer a "buy-it-now" price.

WHEN IS THE BEST TIME TO BUY HARD-TO-GET CONCERT TICKETS? Right after a performer has added extra tour dates. At this time, the supply has usually increased more than the demand. Fewer people tend to want to attend matinee shows and weekday shows, so tickets for those shows will be easier to buy, though unlike matinee movie tickets, they probably won't be any cheaper. **FYI:** Movie tickets are cheaper early in the day— between late morning and late afternoon—because theaters want to attract people who haven't eaten lunch or dinner and will fill up on popcorn, candy, and sodas. The amount of money these theatergoers save on matinee tickets pales in comparison to what they spend on food and drinks.

WHEN IS THE BEST MONTH OF THE YEAR TO BUY NATIONAL FOOTBALL LEAGUE TICKETS? December. Despite the fact that National Football League teams play in stadiums that hold 60,000 or more people, these tickets can be the hardest to get of any professional sport. NFL teams play only sixteen regular-season games—eight at home and eight on the road—compared to professional baseball and basketball teams, which play 162 and 82 regular-season games per season, respectively. Typically, at least half of the NFL teams will have losing records by December and little shot of making the playoffs, so fewer people want to see them play, and this waning demand increases your chances of scoring tickets. If your favorite team is playoff bound, it will be harder to get tickets to see them play, but the fact remains that your chances of getting tickets in cities where teams are out of the playoff chase is much better in December than any other time of the season.

WHICH IS THE BEST MONTH OF THE YEAR TO BUY BICYCLES? January. Some stores discount bikes after the holiday shopping season, in part to make room for new products that arrive in stores in February and March. **Money-saving tip:** Many police and sheriff's departments hold auctions in the spring to sell bicycles that were stolen and never claimed or were used by criminals. Find out if and when your police department does this, get there early to inspect the bicycles, and expect to pay as low as 10 to 25 percent of retail value.

WHEN IS THE BEST TIME OF THE YEAR TO BUY A MOTORCYCLE? January and February. This is true for new and used motorcycles. Sales are the slowest this time of year in most of the country, and many dealers will offer good deals to thin out their inventories. This has a trickle-down effect: People who buy new motorcycles in January and February often will sell their used ones this time of year. **Exception to the rule:** In those parts of the West and the South where it's boiling hot in the summer and no fun to be outside, sales can be slow, causing some dealers to discount motorcycles then. **And finally:** Motorcycle dealers tend to be more passionate about motorcycles than car dealers are about cars, so some of them would rather see motorcycles sit in their showrooms for months than sell them for less than the list price.

WHICH IS THE BEST DAY OF THE WEEK TO BUY A CAR? Tuesday or Wednesday. Shop then and you'll get more attention from the sales staff, especially right after the dealership opens or in the early afternoon. Fewer car buyers shop on weekdays than on Saturdays, reducing the chance that another buyer who wants the car you want is on the lot. The fact that there are fewer shoppers increases the likelihood that dealers will lower prices to sell cars on those days. **Tip:** Make sure you're well rested and fed so you won't be distracted, and you'll be less likely to rush the negotiations.

WHEN IS THE BEST TIME OF THE MONTH TO BUY A CAR? The end. That's when dealerships are most desperate to make their quotas. **Shopping tip:** Consider using the dealer's Web site. You may not save a lot of money, but you'll avoid the high-pressure negotiations in the sales and finance offices.

WHEN IS THE BEST TIME OF THE YEAR TO BUY CARS? The fall. September is when new cars begin arriving at dealerships and when dealers begin discounting older models to make room for the new ones. Expect to save 10 to 20 percent then on the previous year's model. And while September is the best time to buy for those who don't want to risk that someone else will buy the car they want, if you're willing to wait until October, November, and even December, you'll get a better deal. By then dealers are very anxious to clear their lots of older models.

WHEN IS THE BEST TIME TO TELL A NEW CAR SALESMAN YOU HAVE A TRADE-IN? Not until after you've agreed upon a price for the new car. After you've decided which car you want, your first priority should be to negotiate the lowest price you can on the car. Then, and only then, find out what the dealership will give you for the trade-in. Many car salesmen will offer to give you a good price for your trade-in—often as high as or higher than the Blue Book value—in the hopes that you won't be as aggressive in negotiating down the price of the car you want. **Tip:** Know how much your trade-in is worth. If you don't get a good price from the dealer, sell it yourself.

WHEN IS THE BEST TIME TO BUY A BOAT? January to March. This is the winter boat show season, and manufacturers say dealers typically offer their best prices during these shows, where attendees who are already thinking about buying a boat can be convinced by a good price.

WHEN IS THE BEST TIME TO BUY AN RV? Fall and winter. Some of the same logic that applies to cars also applies to recreational vehicles. New models come out in the fall, so you can find good deals on older models then. RV dealers also sometimes offer good prices in the winter to try to boost slumping sales.

WHEN IS THE BEST TIME TO BUY NEW TIRES? When the tread is down to 1/8 inch. The old standard was 1/16 inch, and drivers would gauge that by holding a penny upside down in the tread: If they could see the top of Lincoln's head, they needed new tires. To determine if your tire tread has shrunk to 1/8 inch, do the same thing with a quarter. It's about 1/8 inch from the rim of the coin to George Washington's hairline. If you can see more of his head than that, it could be time to replace your tires.

WHEN IS THE BEST TIME OF THE YEAR TO BUY NEW TIRES? In the fall. As a tire wears out, traction in rain and snow decreases, so in the winter, when you're driving on snow and ice, you need your tires to be at their best.

WHEN IS THE BEST DAY OF THE WEEK TO GET YOUR CAR REPAIRED? Thursday. This seems to be the slowest day of the week for a lot of auto repair shops, and as a result, many shop owners are willing to offer discounts to get work in the door. **Money-saving tips:** You have to ask for that discount if you expect to get it. You're in an even better position to negotiate if you're having more than one repair made to your car.

WHEN IS THE BEST TIME OF THE DAY TO TAKE YOUR CAR IN FOR AN OIL CHANGE? Shortly before closing time. This is especially true of those national chain oil-change businesses, which may lure you in with a good price and then pressure you into having additional repairs done. This is called "upselling," and it can be very annoying. If you arrive at the business early in the day, the technicians and mechanics have more time to look over your vehicle and suggest repairs. If you just want your oil changed, get there in the late afternoon, when the mechanics often are tired and not interested in generating more work for themselves at a time of day when they just want to call it quits.

WHEN IS THE BEST TIME OF DAY TO PUMP GAS? The morning. But it's not why you think, so let's start by debunking a myth: Gasoline may be more dense during the coldest time of the day, but only barely, so those who say you get more for your money by buying gas then are only barely right. The temperature of gas when it is dispensed varies only slightly, and any extra gas you get by pumping in the morning, when it's usually coldest, is so small that it's difficult to measure. The real reason to buy gasoline in the morning? Gas stations often change prices between ten and noon—after gas station managers get instructions from their supervisors or after owner-operators check out prices at competing stations—and these days that means they'll *raise* prices then, not *lower* them. **More gas-saving tips:** 1) Make sure your tires have the right pressure. 2) Use the cheaper regular unleaded fuel whenever you can. 3) Avoid idling for more than a minute and making sudden stops and starts. 4) Don't weigh your car down with things you don't need, especially rooftop carriers, which can cut your mileage by as much as 15 percent. In a test conducted by *Consumer Reports*, a rooftop carrier lowered the gas mileage of a Toyota Camry traveling at 65 mph from 35 miles per gallon to 29. **FYI:** Contrary to popular belief, dirty air filters don't hurt fuel efficiency, at least not on modern engines, which use computers to control the ratio between air and fuel. Even so, air filters do an important job, so don't let them get dirty. **And finally:** Most people know that opening your car windows while you drive creates an aerodynamic drag that slightly reduces gas mileage, but that reduction in gas mileage is the same as if you turn on your air conditioner.

WHICH IS THE BEST DAY OF THE WEEK TO PUMP GAS? Wednesday mornings. This isn't true every week, but prices usually are lowest then. Closer to the weekends, gas prices often rise to pick the pockets of leisure travelers. Prices often begin to rise on Thursdays.

WHEN IS THE BEST TIME TO CONSOLIDATE YOUR CAR AND HOME INSURANCE? As soon as possible, in most cases. Companies offer deep discounts—sometimes as high as 20 percent—for consolidating. Another benefit: only dealing with one agent.

WHICH IS THE BEST MONTH TO BUY A CAMERA? February. Camera makers often release new models in the winter, particularly January and February, when the biggest trade shows of the year occur. Unless you must have the latest and greatest model, February is a great time to camera shop. Wait for the Presidents' Day sales.

WHEN IS THE BEST TIME OF THE YEAR TO BUY SMALL APPLIANCES AND OTHER ELECTRONICS? April and the holidays. April is a good time because the fiscal year for most Japanese manufacturers ends on March 31. That's when they start introducing new models and want to unload the older items. Electronics retailers also tend to lower prices around all of the holidays, even minor ones such as Presidents' Day and Columbus Day. Starting in 2007, many retailers started putting electronics on sale in early November to try to elongate the Christmas shopping season.

WHICH IS THE BEST DAY OF THE YEAR TO BUY ELECTRONICS? On the day after Thanksgiving, known as Black Friday, some retailers drop prices so low that they take a loss on certain items to draw shoppers. Some of these items sell out quickly, and stores don't always offer rain checks, so don't sleep in that day if you've got to have the latest, greatest gadget.

WHICH IS THE BEST MONTH TO BUY A TV? December or January. New TV models, announced at the national Consumer Electronics Show in January, arrive in stores in August and September. Retailers often drop prices for new TVs a few months later, and they also knock down prices on older models. If you need a TV and it's not December or January, do some research and make a list of sets that were introduced six to twelve months ago. Chances are they have dropped in price.

WHICH IS THE BEST MONTH OF THE YEAR TO BUY A REFRIGERATOR? May and sometimes June. You can save hundreds of dollars during this time, when stores usually discount existing refrigerators to make room for new models that arrive in the summer. Sales after the New Year also are not uncommon. **Best day of the week?** Weekdays. The prices aren't better, but stores are less crowded, lines are shorter, and salespeople have more time to spend with customers.

WHEN IS THE BEST TIME OF THE YEAR TO BUY RANGES AND STOVES? Holiday weekends and September and October. Cooking-related appliances typically go on sale around the holidays, especially the Fourth of July and Labor Day. Ranges also get discounted in September and October, when new models arrive. **FYI:** The same usually goes for dishwashers.

WHEN IS THE BEST TIME OF THE YEAR TO BUY AN AIR CONDITIONER? December, January, or February. When it's cool outside, most people aren't thinking about air-conditioning, lowering the demand—and the price, as retailers seek to move merchandise out of their stores. **Keep in mind:** Some stores only stock air conditioners from April through September.

WHEN IS THE BEST TIME TO REPLACE YOUR FURNACE? The spring or the fall. Contractors are busy with emergency heating and cooling calls in the winter and summer, and you're more likely to get a good deal when they're not as busy.

WHEN IS THE BEST MONTH TO BUY A VACUUM CLEANER? April or May. Retailers drop prices then to make room in their stores for new models that come out in June.

WHEN IS THE BEST MONTH TO BUY A COMPUTER? August. Back-to-school sales for computers often offer the lowest prices of the year. Expect savings of $50 and up and freebies, including printers. **The next best time?** It's a tie between winter holiday sales and inventory clearance time in late January and February. Short of that, follow the release schedule for the big chip makers. They often offer clues as to when computer companies will offer updates and redesigns. **Money-saving tip:** Buy computers with slightly older technology, and you won't miss much. You can always upgrade later and still probably come out ahead.

WHEN IS THE BEST MONTH TO BUY MP3 PLAYERS, SUCH AS AN IPOD OR A GIGABEAT? August or September. Some stores put older models on sale then to make room for the models released in September and October, just in time for consumers to get acquainted with them before it's time to buy Christmas and Hanukkah gifts. **The next best time?** January. Look for good sales then, especially if manufacturers' sales expectations for the Christmas season fall short.

WHEN IS THE BEST TIME OF THE YEAR TO BUY VIDEO GAMES? January through March. New video games often come out during the holiday season, but don't expect to find many on sale then. Look for the sales after Christmas. And sometimes there are good sales in the summer, when fewer titles are released.

WHEN IS THE BEST MONTH TO BUY TOYS? October or November. New toys often arrive in stores in September, and retailers will wait a few weeks before lowering prices to try to beat their competitors' prices. Fall is also when stores offer good sales on games, puzzles, and other toys in order to jump-start the holiday shopping season. Getting shoppers in stores in October and November increases the likelihood that they'll return in December for holiday shopping.

WHEN IS THE BEST TIME TO BUY A LIVE CHRISTMAS TREE? Right after Thanksgiving. That's when you're more likely to have your pick of the best-shaped trees with the straightest trunks. If you take your tree down shortly after Christmas, you'll get more for your money if you buy your tree in late November and keep it up for a month. Christmas trees typically stay fresh and smelling great for at least four weeks, but trees bought right before Christmas Day probably were cut several weeks earlier and are more likely to be dry and not as aromatic because their trunks haven't been sitting in water.

WHEN IS THE BEST TIME OF DAY TO GO CHRISTMAS SHOPPING? The earlier in the day, the better. Right after stores open, crowds tend to be lighter, except for Black Friday (the day after Thanksgiving), when the earliest crowds in some stores can be rude and aggressive. But if you can brave the Black Friday crowd, though, you'll find good deals. If you don't like to shop in stores, shop online. Some retail Web sites sometimes offer special discounts only in the morning.

WHEN IS THE BEST TIME TO BUY A GIFT CARD? Right before you give it to someone. Gift card recipients don't always realize that the cards sometimes have expiration dates and dormancy fees. Find out before you buy one. If you still decide to buy it, make sure the person who receives it knows about any restrictions.

WHEN IS THE BEST TIME OF YEAR TO BUY CHRISTMAS CARDS AND WRAPPING PAPER? Right after Christmas. For being brave enough to join the hordes of unsatisfied gift recipients, you'll be rewarded with discounts of 50 percent to 90 percent on Christmas stuff. **Money-saving tip:** Stock up on gold, silver, red, green, and other solid-color paper and ribbons, and use them throughout the year for birthdays, weddings, and anniversaries.

WHEN IS THE BEST TIME OF DAY TO RETURN MERCHANDISE? Ten in the morning. This doesn't apply to December 26, of course, but on any other day, get to the store not long after it opens. It's more likely at this time that staffers are at their assigned posts and that the workers who are there will be in the best position to help you—the best, more experienced workers typically are scheduled to work the day shifts. **FYI:** Many retailers—Ann Taylor, Limited Brands, Gap, and Williams-Sonoma, to name a few—have begun using computer programs to determine when and how many hours sales people should work. Those who sell the most merchandise are assigned to work when stores are busiest, and they get more hours than employees who don't sell as much.

WHEN IS THE BEST TIME OF THE YEAR TO BUY EASTER BASKETS AND DECORATIONS? The week after Easter. Expect discounts of 75 percent or more on those items, which stores will gladly sell at a loss rather than pay to truck them away and store them. This is also a great time for chocolate lovers to pay pennies on the dollar for bunnies that didn't find their way into Easter baskets.

WHEN IS THE BEST TIME TO UPGRADE YOUR CELL PHONE SERVICE? When your contract is up. Your contractor may bend over backward to get you to sign another contract. Make sure your contract allows you to go month to month after it expires, and use that time to get as much as you can out of your current provider or find a new one.

WHEN IS THE BEST TIME TO NEGOTIATE A DISCOUNT? When you have the upper hand. When is that? If you notice a floor model or discounted item isn't selling, you have the upper hand. Same thing on highly competitive services, such as cable TV and newspapers and magazine subscriptions, in which your continued business is especially important. Ask for extras, and make it clear you're ready to take your business elsewhere. Many consumer advocates urge shoppers to haggle even when they don't necessarily have the upper hand. **Tip:** Always talk with the manager or someone who has the authority to lower the price, and if you can't get a lower price on the item, ask for free accessories, delivery, or installation.

WHEN IS THE BEST TIME TO BUY EXTENDED WARRANTIES? Almost never. Salespeople often try to sell them because the profit margins on warranties are very high. They're so high because they're rarely used. Most electronics, for example, have few moving parts that are prone to wear. They don't break for three or four years. If something does break, it typically costs as much to repair it as you paid for the extended warranty. Surveys show, for example, that about one in six refrigerators needs repairs in the first three years, and on average those repair costs are about the cost of the warranty. **Tip:** Buy with a credit card—many gold and platinum cards extend the manufacturer's warranty up to a year for free. **An exception to the rule:** Laptops. Hard drives and screens can fail over time and cost hundreds of dollars or more to replace.

WHEN IS THE BEST TIME TO APPLY FOR A REBATE? As soon as possible. Four out of ten people eligible for rebates never get them because they wait too long or forget to collect the necessary paperwork. If you wait until right before the deadline and then find out you forgot to submit some documentation, you run out of time. Understand the requirements and deadlines.

WHEN IS THE BEST TIME TO BUY BROADWAY TICKETS? A few hours before the show starts, when theaters are most desperate to fill their seats and may offer deep discounts. Don't want to risk getting shut out? Wait in line at the famous TKTS booth near Times Square for half-price tickets, or at the less well-known TKTS booths in downtown Manhattan, by the South Street Seaport Museum, or in downtown Brooklyn, which offer additional ticket discounts, including next-day as well as day-of deals. But do so knowing that you may wait in a long line only to learn when you get to the counter that there are no seats available for the shows you really want to see.

WHICH IS THE BEST DAY OF THE WEEK TO EAT DINNER OUT? Tuesday. Most restaurants don't receive deliveries on Saturdays and Sundays, and many are closed on Mondays. Restaurants that are open on Sundays and Mondays sometimes are cleaning out their refrigerators and serving food that may not be fresh. Food deliveries start early in the week, so the food served on Tuesday is fresh. **Bonus:** Most restaurants aren't crowded that day.

WHICH IS THE BEST DAY OF THE WEEK TO GO GROCERY SHOPPING? Wednesday. Weekly sales at grocery stores almost always start on Wednesdays and end on Tuesdays. If you shop on a Wednesday, it's much less likely that an item you want has sold out. Also, knowing that Wednesdays are the first day of the sale, grocery stores usually are adequately staffed, so you won't have to send out a search party to find an employee to help you find the canned beets. **Another view:** Sunday. Stores usually aren't crowded then—except for right after church services—and you may have just clipped coupons from the newspaper inserts. But don't expect stores to be well stocked or staffed then. **Money-saving tips:** 1) Shopping at night can be a good time to find deep discounts on perishable foods that will be tossed out if they aren't sold by closing time. 2) Whenever you decide to go, don't take your kids, who may pester you to buy things you never would have bought if you were alone. And even if you stick to your guns, saying "no" 47,000 times is bound to make for an unpleasant experience. 3) To reduce impulse buying, make a list and stick to it, and go to the grocery store once a week or even as infrequently two or three times a month. Expect to save about $10 in impulse buys for every trip you don't make.

WHEN IS THE BEST TIME OF THE DAY TO SHOP FOR MEAT? First thing in the morning on week-days. If you go then, you may find "Manager's Specials," which often must be sold by noon that day. Depending on the grocery store chain, expect discounts of 50 percent or more. Just freeze what you won't use right away.

WHEN IS THE BEST TIME TO BUY EGGS? When they're on sale. Right now you're thinking, "Duh!" But here's a neat tidbit that most shoppers don't know: Grocery stores some-times put eggs on sale when they're approaching their expiration dates and must be sold. For most perishables, expiration dates signify the last day they should be eaten. Not so with eggs, which can be eaten three to five weeks after the expiration date.

WHEN IS THE BEST TIME OF THE DAY TO BUY BREAD AND OTHER FRESH-BAKED GOODS? Late afternoon and into the evening. Many grocery stores with bakery departments start discounting their fresh bread by 50 percent around 4 p.m. because bakery department managers don't want to throw anything away at the end of the day. Half-price discounts are common. Of course, you can buy bread for about half price any day at discount bread stores, but it's less fresh than what you'll get at grocery store bakeries. **Money-saving tip:** Many dollar stores now sell name-brand sliced bread, buns, bagels, and English muffins, which sell for $2.50 and up at grocery stores.

WHEN IS THE BEST DAY OF THE WEEK TO BUY FRESH FISH AT A SEAFOOD MARKET? Any day but Monday. Fishermen typically work Mondays through Saturdays, with only Sundays off.

So the fish you buy on a Monday probably was caught on a Saturday or maybe even a Friday, and the fish you buy on other days probably was caught twenty-four hours or less before you bought it. **Tips:** When shopping for whole fish, look for bright, clear eyes, shiny scales, bright red gills, and an odor of clean water. Avoid dull eyes, brick red gills, and fishy-smelling fish. Fillets should also have shiny skin and a clean-water smell, and the liquid you see in the packaging should be clear, not milky.

WHEN IS THE BEST TIME TO USE COUPONS? When they're for items you usually buy. Always use coupons for staples, such as ketchup, toilet paper, margarine, and cereal. If you don't have to drive too far, buy at least some of your groceries at grocery stores that double your coupons. **Money-saving tip:** Avoid using coupons for frozen foods and other high-priced items you usually don't buy, but if you have a coupon for an item you've always wanted to try and that item is also on sale, go ahead and buy it.

WHEN IS THE BEST TIME TO BUY CONDIMENTS, SALAD DRESSINGS, NAPKINS, AND OTHER THINGS YOU MIGHT NEED AT A SUMMER BARBECUE? Mid-May to early June. Companies that sell these products often offer deep discounts this time of year, hoping you'll stock up and have no need to buy their competitors' products all summer long. **Money-saving tip:** Go one better and buy a year's worth of these items. Sauces and salad dressings store safely for at least a year.

WHEN IS THE BEST TIME OF THE YEAR TO BUY FROZEN TURKEYS? After the holidays. Some grocers will lower the price of turkeys before Thanksgiving and Christmas to attract shoppers, but the best prices are right after the holidays, when grocers are trying to get rid of unsold turkeys, which take up a lot of space in their frozen-food cases.

WHICH IS THE BEST MONTH TO BUY BUTTER AND OTHER DAIRY PRODUCTS? June or July, when production is up and prices often are down. Stock up on butter then. You can freeze it and use it until the end of the year or even into the next year.

WHICH IS THE BEST MONTH TO BUY FROZEN FOODS? March. It's National Frozen Food Month, an invention of the National Frozen and Refrigerated Foods Association, a trade group that, among other things, encourages the distribution of frozen food coupons in March. So you're likely to get good deals then. **The next best month?** November. That's when stores try to lure shoppers into their stores to stock up on pies and other frozen foods they'll eat at holiday meals.

WHEN IS THE BEST TIME OF THE YEAR TO BUY FRESH FRUITS? When they're in season. The flavors are at their peak, and the prices are usually lower then because they're more plentiful and grocers don't want to see them rot in the stores. The U.S. Department of Agriculture claims you can eat three servings of fruit and four servings of vegetables a day for less than a dollar. Most fruits are available year-round, but here's an incomplete list of when fruits are at their peak—and should cost less:

JANUARY: cranberries, grapefruit, oranges, and tangerines
FEBRUARY: grapefruit and oranges
MARCH: grapefruit, oranges, pineapple, and strawberries
APRIL: grapefruit, oranges, pineapples, and strawberries
MAY: blackberries, blueberries, cantaloupe, cherries, grapefruit, honeydew melons, oranges, peaches, pineapples, and strawberries
JUNE: apricots, blackberries, blueberries, cantaloupe, cherries, honeydew melons,

limes, nectarines, oranges, peaches, pineapples, plums, strawberries, and watermelons

JULY: apricots, blackberries, blueberries, cantaloupe, cherries, honeydew melons, limes,
nectarines, peaches, plums, strawberries, and watermelons

AUGUST: blueberries, cantaloupe, cherries, honeydew melons, limes, nectarines,peaches,
Bartlett pears, plums, raspberries, and watermelons

SEPTEMBER: apples, blueberries, cantaloupe, cranberries, honeydew melons, nectarines, peaches, Bartlett pears, and plums

OCTOBER: apples, cranberries, honeydew melons, oranges, peaches, and Bartlett pears

NOVEMBER: apples, cranberries, grapefruit, honeydew melons, oranges, Bartlett pears,
and tangerines

DECEMBER: apples, cranberries, grapefruit, oranges, and tangerines
Avocados, bananas, grapes, and lemons cost roughly the same year round.

WHEN IS THE BEST TIME OF YEAR TO BUY FRESH VEGETABLES? Again, when they're in season,
and for all the reasons it makes sense to buy fresh fruits when they're in season. Here's a
short list of vegetables in their prime season:

JANUARY: cabbage, cauliflower, and rhubarb

FEBRUARY: cauliflower and rhubarb

MARCH: broccoli and rhubarb

APRIL: artichokes, asparagus, broccoli, green onions, lettuce, peas, rhubarb, and
spinach

MAY: artichokes, asparagus, broccoli, corn, green onions, lettuce, peas, radishes,
rhubarb, and spinach

JUNE: corn, cucumbers, lettuce, and radishes

JULY: corn, cucumbers, lettuce, and radishes

AUGUST: corn, cucumbers, eggplants, lettuce, and peppers

SEPTEMBER: cauliflower, corn, eggplants, peppers, and spinach

OCTOBER: broccoli, Brussels sprouts, cauliflower, and spinach

NOVEMBER: broccoli, Brussels sprouts, cauliflower, mushrooms, and spinach

DECEMBER: broccoli, Brussels sprouts, cauliflower, and mushrooms

WHEN IS THE BEST TIME OF DAY TO GET A GOOD DEAL AT A FARMERS' MARKET? Right before it closes. Sellers dread having to pack up their trucks with produce and flowers and whatever else they've got, so that's when they offer the best deals of the day. This is also why closing time is the best time to find a good deal at a garage sale, but it's even more true at a farmers' market. Many of the products sold there are perishable and might be too old to sell the next day.

WHEN IS THE BEST TIME OF THE YEAR TO BUY BOTTLED WATER? The summer. To increase traffic, stores often drop the price of bottled water during the summer, when they know shoppers are going to picnics and barbecues. If you've become addicted to bottled water, summer is a great time to stock up on it. If you are addicted, you're not alone. Americans spend about $15 billion a year on bottled water, 44 percent of which comes from the same municipal sources that give you your tap water. **FYI:** To see how safe your tap water is, read the drinking water quality report, also known as the consumer confidence report, that your water provider must send you every year by July 1 and post online. **Money-saving tips:** Buy a twelve-pack of bottled water, and as you drink it, save the empty bottles and the caps. At night, before you go to bed, fill a large pitcher with tap water and let it sit out uncovered on your counter overnight. The odor from the chemicals used to make the water drinkable—if there is any—will evaporate. In the morning, fill your empty plastic bottles with the water from the pitcher, cap them, and take them with you. Still don't like the taste? Buy a filter for your kitchen faucet. How much money will you save? A lot. Let's say you find a case of water at the grocery store for $5, or about $1.25 per gallon. Water from the tap—and even filtered tap water—costs less than one cent per gallon.

WHICH IS THE BEST MONTH TO BUY CHAMPAGNE? December. With the demand for Champagne increasing as New Year's Eve gets closer, it would be logical to assume this would be the worst month to buy Champagne. But competition between Champagne producers is so fierce during this time of year that many stores can lower prices and put the bubbly on sale in December.

WHEN IS THE BEST TIME OF YEAR TO BUY WINE? The fall. The fall harvest season, when most vineyards release their latest vintages, offers the best selection. August and September are the best months to buy popular "cult wines," which usually are made in limited numbers and can't be found later in the year.

WHEN IS THE BEST MONTH TO BUY COOKWARE? April, May, October, or November. There are two big seasons for cookware: The spring season coincides with graduations and weddings, and the fall season with the end-of-the-year holidays. If you can wait for one of these seasons, you'll find good sales.

WHEN IS THE BEST TIME OF THE YEAR TO BUY A CHARCOAL GRILL? After Labor Day. Sales of as much as 30 percent off start then and continue through December, but you'll find the best selection in September and October. **How about gas grills?** December. Gas grills also drop in price after the summer, but they cost more than charcoal grills and store managers usually tolerate their presence in their stores longer. Most people buy them in the spring and summer. Wait until the end of the year when demand is at a low point.

WHEN IS THE BEST TIME OF THE YEAR TO BUY TREES AND SHRUBS? The fall. Nurseries drop prices after the summer as they try to clear out their stock. **Money-saving tip:** Buy bulbs in the fall, store them in the winter, and plant them in the spring.

WHICH IS THE BEST MONTH TO BUY TOOLS? June. Stores often lower prices on selected tools the week before Father's Day to lure shoppers. **Another view:** As soon as possible. Tools are one of those things that never really get much cheaper if you wait to buy them. A hammer or a saw or a drill costs more this year than it cost last year and will likely cost more next year.

WHEN IS THE BEST TIME TO BUY LAWN MOWERS? The fall. Actually, starting in August mom-and-pop stores and the big-box retailers start putting lawn mowers on sale to make room for large fall and winter items, such as leaf machines and snowblowers. Expect discounts of at least 10 percent in August and as much as 40 percent in November, when stores are really getting desperate. Still can't afford that riding lawn mower you've had your eye on all summer long? Consider taking out a loan. That mower very well may cost $500 more if you wait until the spring, and the $500 you'll save by buying it now promises to exceed whatever interest you pay on the loan.

WHICH IS THE BEST MONTH TO BUY SNOWBLOWERS? March. Lowe's, Home Depot, and other home improvement stores don't want these in their stores or warehouses in the spring and summer, so they and other retailers start discounting them just before winter ends—late February and March in much of the country. The only downside is that you'll have to find a place in your garage to store it for eight or nine months before the first time you'll use it.

WHICH IS THE BEST MONTH OF THE YEAR TO BUY PAINT? January or the summer. You can find sales on paint year round, but there are lots of sales in January, when home-improvement and other stores try to lure shoppers who wouldn't necessarily think of taking on a painting project during the winter. Why the summer? The opposite reason: Stores know more people paint during the warm months, so they sometimes lower prices then, counting on you to buy additional full-priced items you didn't know you were looking for.

WHEN IS THE BEST TIME TO BUY FURNITURE? January and July. Buyers can expect the lowest prices of the years during these months because retailers are trying to make room for new models, which arrive in February and August. There's nothing wrong with the older models. In fact, often the newer ones have the same frames with different upholstery in different colors.

WHEN IS THE BEST TIME TO BUY LINENS AND BEDDING? January. The white sale was a marketing strategy devised by John Wanamaker in 1878, and it was so successful that retailers still follow his lead today. Major department stores still discount their wares in January because that's when they tend to do their annual inventory. And many catalogers often follow suit. For those who miss the January white sales, new linens come out seasonally, so there are always opportunities to get good deals on winter linens in the spring, spring linens in the summer, and so on.

WHEN IS THE BEST TIME TO BUY A NEW PILLOW? Every two years. This is especially true if you're allergic to dust mites, those pesky critters that live in pillows, mattresses, and clothing. If you're not allergic, you don't have to buy a new pillow as often, unless the thought of these microscopic creatures sharing your bed bugs you. **Money-saving tip:** Don't buy a new pillow if the one you're using is still comfortable. Just wash it in hot water (about 120 degrees F) or put it in the freezer. Dust mites can't survive in extreme temperatures.

WHEN IS THE BEST TIME OF THE YEAR TO BUY A PROM DRESS? January and February. New styles show up in stores then, and selection is the largest. The most popular styles typically sell out long before prom season, and shopping early also gives you plenty of time to have the dress altered. **Money-saving tip:** Check thrift stores and your mother and older sisters' closets, which can be great places to find dresses that none of your friends will be wearing on prom night.

WHEN IS THE BEST TIME OF THE YEAR TO BUY A WEDDING DRESS? Between Thanksgiving and Christmas. Bridal shops stock up on dresses in November because so many people get engaged at Christmas and New Year's. Many brides-to-be postpone shopping for their dresses until January or February, but if you shop in December when stores are less crowded and are trying to boost their end-of-the-year sales, you'll be in a better position to negotiate.

WHEN IS THE BEST TIME OF THE WEEK TO SAVE MONEY ON YOUR WEDDING? Weeknights and Sundays. The vast majority of weddings take place on Saturdays, so if you're willing to buck that trend, you may be able to save a lot of money, especially from wedding venue managers who would rather their halls not go unused. **One more tip:** If your wedding ceremony will be in a church, consider scheduling it just before Easter or Christmas. The church will already be decorated, and you'll save lots of money on flowers.

WHEN IS THE BEST TIME OF THE YEAR TO SAVE MONEY ON YOUR WEDDING? Winter. If you're all about saving money, forget about that June wedding, when demand for halls, flowers, and other wedding-related needs are high—and so are the prices. Try the winter, when demand and prices are lower.

WHEN IS THE BEST MONTH TO BUY JEWELRY? January, March, April, July, August, or September—otherwise known as the non–gift giving months. Prices go up in February for Valentine's Day, May for Mother's Day, and June for graduations, Father's Day, and weddings. October, November, and December are the months in which shoppers buy for the end-of-the-year holidays, and they're also the months in which jewelers tend to make the vast majority of their profits. You're more likely to pay full price in December as well as the weeks before Valentine's Day and Mother's Day. The non–gift giving months are when you're more likely to see *real* sales, as opposed to the jewelry that gets marked up in anticipation of Valentine's Day, Mother's Day, and Christmas and then put on sale.

WHEN IS THE BEST TIME TO SELL JEWELRY? When you don't really need the money. The more desperate the sellers are for money, the less money buyers, such as jewelers and pawn shop owners, will pay for it. How small are the offers? As little as 50 percent of wholesale. **Tip:** Figure out how much your jewelry is worth before you sell it, and remember that, despite a high appraisal, it's ultimately only worth as much as a buyer is willing to pay for it.

WHEN IS THE BEST TIME TO BUY GOLD? When the economy is stable. That's when gold prices are lower. During a recession or a period of economic instability, the dollar decreases in value, and people tend to look to gold as an investment. The demand for gold drives up the price, and it's not as good a deal then. Some gold investors point out that the value, or buying power, of gold hasn't changed in more than 200 years. That means if you paid for a horse in the year 1809 with an ounce of gold, you could buy a horse in 2009 with an ounce of gold. (Gold price in 1808: $19 an ounce; in 2009: about $900 an ounce.)

WHEN IS THE BEST TIME OF THE YEAR TO BUY A HORSE? The fall. This was more true years ago when the country was more agrarian, but some summer camps and tourist operations will sell their horses at the end of the season, and many can be had for a good price. What's more, some horse owners who don't ride much in the winter will sell in the fall for less than they would in the spring and summer to avoid paying to feed and board their horses all winter. Thoroughbreds sometimes go on sale for a good price at the end of the racing season, but bear in mind that they can be high-strung and difficult to retrain. And buying your little princess a pony for Christmas usually isn't a good idea for the same reason it isn't a good idea to buy any pet during that hectic time of the year. **The bottom line:** Buy a horse when you know you can give it the attention it deserves.

CHAPTER TWO

TO-DO LIST

Shopaholics may disagree, but there's more to life than spending money. Think of how much time you could save and how productive you'd be if you knew the best time to *do* things. In this chapter, you'll learn the best time to have your picture taken, potty train your youngster, walk your dog, jog, go to the post office, eat a snack, get a tattoo or a haircut, kill dandelions or wasps, and much more. And you may think you don't care, but trust me—after you find out what gets thrown away, you'll want to know the best time to Dumpster dive.

WHEN IS THE BEST TIME TO DO THE MOST DIFFICULT TASKS OF THE DAY? Between 10 a.m. and 11 a.m. While you sleep, the stress hormone cortisol rises, increasing your blood sugar and giving you enough energy to manage difficult situations effectively about three hours after you wake up, during the late morning. This is a time of day when you are most alert and feel like you're up to just about any challenge.

WHEN IS THE BEST TIME OF THE DAY TO TAKE A NAP? Early afternoon. But eating a big lunch has nothing to do with it. Doctors have found that in the early afternoon, your body temperature dips, causing sleepiness. Early afternoon is also when your circadian rhythms—the pattern of physical and mental changes we repeat every twenty-four hours—trigger sleepiness. Many doctors point out that people who get enough undisturbed sleep at night don't need naps in the afternoon, or any other time of the day, for that matter. But some doctors say midday naps will help you function better even if you slept well the night before. In fact, a NASA study found that a twenty-six-minute nap improved pilots' performance by 34 percent. **The worst time?** After 3 p.m. Napping that late in the day may make it more difficult to fall asleep that night. **Tips:** 1) Don't nap for more than an hour at a time—that can sap your energy. 2) If you started your day without enough sleep and you know you won't have time to nap that afternoon, make sure your lunch includes foods packed with lots of protein, which will give you plenty of energy to make it through the day.

WHEN IS THE BEST TIME TO WRITE POETRY? Teens and twenties. The energy, enthusiasm, and passion that accompany youth can create great poetry, according to researchers who specialize in creativity. One said, "Lyric poetry is a domain where talent is discovered early, burns brightly, and then peters out at an early age." These researchers point to T. S. Eliot, who at twenty-three wrote the groundbreaking "The Love Song of J. Alfred Prufrock," and to Frenchman Arthur Rimbaud, dubbed "an infant Shakespeare," who wrote critically acclaimed poetry through his teen years, then stopped creative writing at twenty-one.

WHEN IS THE BEST TIME OF THE DAY TO PLAY A MUSICAL INSTRUMENT? Late afternoon. Hand-eye coordination reaches optimal levels then. It's also a time when most people report being fairly alert, so if your child is learning how to play the guitar, the piano, or some other instrument, try to schedule their lessons after they get out of school.

WHEN IS THE BEST TIME OF THE DAY TO HAVE YOUR PICTURE TAKEN? Late morning or early afternoon. Having your picture taken then gives you a few hours or more to shake off the puffiness from your night of sleep. But don't pose after 3 p.m., when you'll start looking tired from the day's events.

WHEN IS THE BEST TIME OF THE DAY TO TAKE A LANDSCAPE PHOTOGRAPH? Sunrise and sunset. Proper lighting is crucial for photography in general, and for landscape photography, sunrise and sunset are when a wide variety of lighting conditions are available for one or two hours. When the sun is low in the sky, it projects a soft, golden light that highlights colors and shadows, and flatters almost any landscape. During dawn and dusk, you also can shoot right into the sun. **The worst time?** Midday, when the sun is high in the sky and shadows are practically nonexistent.

WHEN IS THE BEST TIME TO VIEW THE MOON THROUGH A TELESCOPE? When it's a half moon. At that time, you'll get a great view of the lunar landscape, including sunlit mountains. As tempting as it may be, don't waste your time with full moons, which can be almost blindingly bright and look flat and one dimensional.

WHEN IS THE BEST MONTH TO SEE THE NORTHERN LIGHTS? March or September. This is especially true if you're in Alaska, the best place by far to see the lights in the United States because they pass right over that state. There are a few good reasons why March and

September are the best months to see the lights, a.k.a. aurora borealis: 1) Solar activity is greatest in Earth's orbit then, and March and September are the most frequent months for auroras; 2) the skies are darkest in March and September, making the lights easier to see; and 3) temperatures usually are mild this time of year, at least by Alaska standards, so you won't freeze as much when you're stargazing.

WHEN IS THE BEST TIME OF DAY TO WATCH THE PERSEID METEOR SHOWER? Early morning when the sky is dark. There are about fifteen recognized meteor showers a year, but the Perseid shower, which is brightest from August 8 through 14, is the most popular because it's biggest, with sixty or more meteors visible per hour. The Perseid shower, so called because it appears to come from the constellation Perseus, has been observed for more than 2,000 years, mostly in the Northern Hemisphere. It usually peaks on August 12, when the shower's largest stream of dust and rock enter Earth's atmosphere and burn up, making the bright streaks in the sky that you see. **Viewing tips:** Check the weather forecast and hope for a clear, moonless sky, then make sure you're far away from city lights and smog.

WHEN IS THE BEST TIME TO HAVE A BABY SHOWER? Four to six weeks before the due date. By this time in the pregnancy, it's less likely that the expectant mother will miscarry, and she'll have plenty of time to incorporate the gifts into her nursery and the rest of her house. And if she receives gift cards, she'll still have lots of time to buy what she needs before the baby arrives. **An exception to this rule:** If the baby is due early in the year, four to six weeks before may fall between Thanksgiving Day and New Year's Day, so you might want to consider having the baby shower earlier—perhaps in the middle of November—or after the holidays. The guests will understand and even appreciate it.

WHEN IS THE BEST TIME TO ASK SOMEONE OUT ON A DATE? Noon. Our moods are often good then because we're looking forward to a well-deserved break in the workday and our minds are less cluttered because we're focusing not on working but on eating. Ask your would-be boyfriend or girlfriend out then. And if you get turned down? That's okay— feelings of depression tend to peak earlier in the day and fade by lunchtime.

WHEN IS THE BEST TIME OF THE DAY TO MAKE LOVE? Between ten at night and one in the morning. Both social and biological factors influence this. First, the biology: Our sense of touch and our skin sensitivity are at their highest levels in the late evening, when we're already in a comfy place—bed. The other reasons, the social ones, tend to be more practical: Couples work during the day and are busy in the early evening, preparing dinner and spending time with their children. Late evening is probably the only time during the week that couples with children can make time for sex. But that isn't the only explanation. During the weekends and on vacations, when our weekday schedules are thrown off, sex still seems to occur more often between 10 p.m. and 1 a.m. **Did you know?** A survey of sex therapists found that three to seven minutes of intercourse is okay, seven to thirteen minutes is ideal, and more than thirteen minutes is too much for most people.

WHERE IN THE ORDER OF SIBLINGS IS IT BEST TO BE BORN? First. New research confirms what other studies have found—that firstborns spend about 3,000 more hours with their parents between the ages of four and thirteen than do their younger siblings during that time. The study concludes that this additional time with firstborns helps explain why so many of them do so well later in life. **Did you know?** More of the time parents spend with their other children is spent watching TV.

WHAT IS THE BEST AGE AT WHICH TO POTTY TRAIN YOUR KIDS? Eighteen to thirty months old. Very few children—maybe two or three out of one hundred—are ready to forgo diapers before eighteen months, and potty training becomes more difficult, though far from impossible, after thirty months. Pediatricians say the eighteen- to thirty-month-old range makes a window during which the vast majority of children show signs of being interested in using the toilet. Some of these signs include wanting to sit on the toilet and wear "big kid" underpants, and being able to identify their private parts and pull their pants up and down by themselves. **The best season?** Summer. Fewer clothes are worn then, and that makes it easier for your child to get his pants down in time. A lot of people say the best window of opportunity is the summer after your child turns two.

WHEN IS THE BEST TIME TO PUT A TV IN YOUR CHILD'S BEDROOM? Never. Various studies have found that children with TVs in their bedrooms are more likely to be overweight, smoke, score lower on tests, and have trouble sleeping. Oh, yeah, and they also watch a lot more TV than do children without TVs in their rooms. A study of eighty children ages four to seven in Buffalo, New York, showed that having a TV in the bedroom increased viewing time from twenty-one hours a week to thirty hours. Children who had time limits on TV viewing didn't necessarily exercise more, but they snacked less, eating about one hundred fewer calories a day than children with no limits. Plenty of other studies also show negative results. In a study of children in six Northern California schools, 70 percent of the students had TVs in their rooms, and as a group they scored lower on math, reading, and language arts tests. Another study of more than 700 students ages twelve to fourteen found that 42 percent of those with TVs in their rooms smoked, compared with 16 percent for kids without TVs in their rooms.

WHEN IS THE BEST TIME TO REWARD OR DISCIPLINE YOUR DOG? No more than thirty seconds after he does something laudable or punishable. That's about how long the act registers with the dog. So if you wait a minute or two to reward your dog after he fetches the newspaper, he won't know why he got a treat. And if you come home from work and find that she's soiled the rug, she certainly won't know why you banished her to the basement.

WHEN IS THE BEST TIME TO TAKE YOUR DOG FOR A WALK? Between 8 p.m. and 9 p.m. You usually have the most time then, which allows your dog to linger and enjoy the walk, compared with the morning walk, which often is rushed because you need to get to work or get the kids off to school. It tends to be cooler in the evening, so walking your dog then also allows him to avoid overheating and wearing himself out before bedtime.

WHEN IS THE BEST TIME OF THE DAY TO TAKE A BREAK FROM YOUR CAT OR DOG? From 11 p.m. to 7 a.m., or whenever you like to sleep. A recent hospital survey found that 53 percent of patients with pets reported that their pets disturbed their sleep every single night, causing them to feel tired during the day. Close your bedroom door, or teach your pet to sleep in a different room. **Did you know?** Doctors and sleep researchers say getting exactly seven and a half hours of sleep a night helps you store that day's information in your memory bank.

WHEN IS THE BEST TIME TO ADOPT A PET? When you can give it the time it deserves. Dogs especially need your time, as they like to exercise and play. **The worst times?** When your workload or school work is heavy or if you're caring for an ailing relative. Living with a new pet can be stressful, so don't make the mistake of taking in a cat or dog if you're going through a divorce and looking for some loyal companionship. **FYI:** A study of 4,435 people who were tracked for twenty years concluded that cat owners were 40 percent

less likely to die of a heart attack than people who live without cats. Why? Researchers don't know for sure, but they speculate that cats offer stress relief. They caution, however, that owning a cat is no substitute for eating right and exercising regularly. By the way, other research has suggested that dogs have the same effect, but not enough people in this study owned dogs for researchers to draw that conclusion.

WHEN IS THE BEST TIME OF THE DAY TO WORK ON A CROSSWORD PUZZLE? Between 10 a.m. and 11 a.m. Studies show this is the time of day when most people—night owls being the exception—say they are most alert, and they feel that they are at their peak intellectually. So if you're doing a crossword puzzle during the late morning, go ahead and use a pen.

WHEN IS THE BEST TIME OF THE DAY TO PLAY VIDEO GAMES? Late afternoon. Hand-eye coordination reaches optimal levels then. **Did you know:** One study found that when performing laparoscopic surgeries, which use a tiny camera and long instruments inserted through small incisions, surgeons who played video games as children made fewer mistakes than surgeons who did not. Another study found that surgeons who played video games to warm up for laparoscopic surgeries performed the surgery faster and made fewer mistakes than those who did not. Why? The researchers concluded that video games sharpen hand-eye coordination, reaction time, and visual skills.

WHEN IS THE BEST TIME OF THE DAY TO GO FOR A RUN? Between 6 p.m. and 8 p.m. Your body temperature is highest then, and it's also the peak time for flexibility, muscle strength, and isometric strength in your knees. During the mid-1980s, Britain's best middle-distance runners—Sebastian Coe, Steve Ovett, Steve Cram, and David Moorcroft—broke several world records, all in the evening. It's true that many of the track meets at which these records were broken were scheduled during this time to increase TV viewership, but trainers, coaches, and doctors attribute at least part of their success to these biological factors.

WHEN IS THE BEST TIME OF THE DAY TO LIFT WEIGHTS? Six in the evening. This is when your muscles have the most potential to perform at their peak, because they're warm and are ready to be tested. And it may help explain why gyms and health clubs often are crowded after work. Trainers say if you notice you're lifting more weight at a certain time of day, that's when you'll want to be at the gym.

WHEN IS THE BEST TIME OF THE DAY TO PLAY FOOTBALL? Starting at 6 p.m. This is when your lungs use oxygen more efficiently, you're more coordinated, and your muscles have the most potential to perform at their peak. In a study by researchers examining the results of twenty-five years of NFL Monday night games, they found the opposite of what you might expect: West Coast teams traveling east were not at a disadvantage because of jet lag. In fact, they won more often and by more points than did East Coast home teams, and they often beat the Las Vegas point spread. The researchers concluded that the West Coast teams did so well because, when the ball was kicked off at shortly after 9 p.m. EST, it felt like 6 p.m. to them. By the time the games ended—usually after midnight—the East Coast teams were playing at a time when their bodies were near the lowest point of athletic performance, but the players on the West Coast teams felt like it was 9 p.m.

WHEN IS THE BEST TIME OF THE DAY TO SWIM FAST? The evening. That's according to British researchers who timed short-distance swimmers throughout the day and found that they swam 100-meter races 2.7 seconds faster at 10 p.m. than at 6:30 a.m. The time difference shocked them, and they can't explain it precisely, but they said the rise in body temperature at night has a significant effect on muscle efficiency. (This doesn't apply as much to elite swimmers, as evidenced by the 2008 Olympians, who swam in the morning and broke world records twenty-five times.) Other researchers have concluded that some swimmers with great potential likely have quit the sport out of frustration because swimmers are known for rigorous practices in the early morning, a time when they are less likely to do well.

WHEN IS THE BEST TIME TO CLEAN YOUR HOUSE? Beginning at 4 p.m. Start then because energy and mood levels typically are high in the late afternoon. **The worst time?** Early afternoon. That's when a dip in body temperature and your circadian rhythms—the pattern of physical and mental changes we repeat every twenty-four hours—trigger sleepiness. **Did you know?** Husbands create an additional seven hours of housework per week for wives.

WHEN IS THE BEST TIME TO PAINT YOUR HOUSE? When temperatures are between 60 and 85 degrees F. That doesn't mean you can't paint when it's a bit cooler or hotter; some paints also work well when temps are as low as the 40s or as hot as the 90s. **Tip:** Whenever possible, paint in the shade. If the sun is beating down on the side of the house you're painting, it can cause even the highest quality paints to blister.

WHICH IS THE BEST MONTH OF THE YEAR TO START A HOME RENOVATION PROJECT OR AN ADDITION? January. This answer depends on the size of the project and other factors, but most homeowners want their houses looking good for Thanksgiving and the end-of-the-year holidays and don't want to start a project that can't be finished before then, so that rules out November and December. And many builders don't want to start a project toward the end of the year because it can be difficult to get materials delivered and find enough workers. Because November and December typically are slow months, builders badly want to work in January. Like you, they have credit card bills from the holidays that arrive in the middle of January. If you can afford to, write what may be the first of many big checks in January. That's the month when you're most likely to have your builder's undivided attention and when you very well may pay less. Not only are lumber and other material costs a bit lower early in the year because of reduced demand, but builders who want your job will make more of an effort this time of year to underbid their competitors.

WHEN IS THE BEST TIME OF THE WEEK TO MOVE YOUR HOUSEHOLD? Mondays through Thursdays. Many families find it more convenient to move on the weekends, so many moving companies, taking advantage of the demand for their services, charge more on the weekends and less to move during the week. Some even advertise discounts to move your things during the week.

WHEN IS THE BEST TIME OF THE MONTH TO MOVE? The middle. This is also driven by supply and demand. Apartment leases in particular are more likely to start at the beginning of a month and end at the end, forcing renters to move at the end of one month in order to be in their next apartment at the beginning of the next. Some moving companies will charge a premium for working then and, conversely, will give a discount to people who move during the middle of the month, when often there is a lull.

WHEN IS THE BEST TIME OF THE YEAR TO MOVE? Anytime but the summer. Real estate professionals and others who track closing dates say as many as 60 percent of everyone who moves from one household to another in a given year does so in the summer. If you're moving during another time of the year and you're doing the backbreaking work yourself, you'll have a larger selection of trucks, and they should cost less to rent.

WHEN IS THE BEST TIME OF DAY TO GO TO THE POST OFFICE? Thirty minutes after your post office opens. If you go then, you'll avoid the early birds who line up at the door, and you'll still get your post office errand out of the way fairly early in the day. **The busiest times?** At lunch and just before closing. Postal officials suggest using USPS "contract stations" that offer services in supermarkets and other stores.

WHEN'S THE BEST TIME OF THE DAY TO HAVE A PRESCRIPTION FILLED? Late morning. The busiest times at most pharmacies tend to be right after they open, during the lunch hour, and after 4 p.m., when lots of people start getting off work. There tends to be a lull from about 10 a.m. to noon, and again from 2 p.m. to 4 p.m., but the lull is more pronounced in the morning because as the day wears on, more people see their doctors and head to drugstores to drop off and pick up their prescriptions. **Tip:** If you're satisfied with the service and cost of the medicine at your pharmacy, don't stray. If you stay with one pharmacy, the pharmacists there will become familiar with your family's history and will be in a better position to catch mistakes.

WHEN IS THE BEST TIME OF THE DAY AND WEEK TO GO TO THE BANK? Midmorning and midweek. Avoid the busiest times, which are right after the bank opens, during the lunch hour, and when people start getting off work. And stay away on Mondays and Fridays, often the busiest banking days of the week. **The worst day?** Friday. Payday brings out folks who want to cash or deposit their paychecks, and it also brings out the folks who want to steal that money. Bank robberies are most likely to occur between 9 a.m. and 11 a.m. on Fridays, according to FBI statistics, because many robbers assume banks have the most money on hand at that time for workers who want to cash their checks. The FBI says that although banks once did have more cash on Fridays, today that assumption is probably more a perception than reality.

WHEN IS THE BEST TIME TO GO TO A DEPARTMENT OF MOTOR VEHICLE OFFICE? Again, think middle. Midmorning, midafternoon, middle of the week, and middle of the month. The worst time of the month is the end, when driver's licenses and vehicle registrations expire. The worst day of the week is Saturday, because many people are off work then and have the time to go. Mondays are also hectic because some people want to get their trip to the DMV over with early in the week. The worst time of the day is the morning, for the same reason that Mondays are busy, so go in the middle of the week if possible, after the morning rush or sometime between lunch and the after-work rush.

WHICH IS THE BEST DAY OF THE YEAR TO VISIT A SOCIAL SECURITY OFFICE? The day after Thanksgiving Day. Very few people seem to know that the agency's local offices are open on the day after Thanksgiving, and because so many people go Christmas shopping on that day, Social Security offices are not busy places then. You're likely to get more time and attention from staffers.

WHEN IS THE BEST TIME OF THE DAY TO GET THROUGH TO A HUMAN BEING AT YOUR PHONE, CABLE, INTERNET, AND POWER COMPANIES? Eight o'clock in the morning, or whenever they open the phone lines. Surprised? Conventional wisdom says that utility companies are flooded with calls then from angry or anxious customers who couldn't get through the day before. But many people on the receiving end of those calls point out that the morning often is a hectic time for their customers, and at 8 a.m., they are either at work, on their way to work, or are preparing to leave for work, or they're trying to get their kids ready for school or taking them there. **The worst time of the day?** Pretty much any other time. **The worst day?** Mondays generally are bad, but the Monday after a Friday holiday is the worst. On those Mondays, some people have been waiting three days to call, and it can take hours to get through, so if you don't have to call that day, wait until first thing Tuesday morning.

WHEN IS THE BEST TIME TO EAT DINNER? Three hours before you go to sleep. You'll sleep better when you allow for at least three hours of digestion to occur, and it's less likely you'll get heartburn at night. **Did you know:** A few studies have tried to determine whether eating most of your calories at night causes weight gain, but all have been inconclusive.

WHEN IS THE BEST TIME OF DAY TO EAT SPICY FOOD? At lunch. Sweet and sour flavors found in Thai and other spicy foods stimulate alertness. That will combat the desire we have to nap in the early afternoon caused by a dip in body temperature and by circadian rhythms—the pattern of physical and mental changes we repeat every twenty-four hours. **The worst time?** Right before bedtime. Plenty of research supports the old wives' tale that you should avoid spicy food right before sleeping. In one study, Australian researchers fed a group of healthy young men food with mustard and Tabasco sauce shortly before bedtime and found that they took longer to fall asleep and slept less. The researchers attribute this to indigestion and higher body temperatures, which have been linked to less sleep.

WHEN IS THE BEST TIME OF DAY TO HAVE A SNACK? Around 3 p.m. There's nothing wrong with snacks as long as they're not too close to dinner time. But stay away from chips and chocolate bars. Nuts and other snacks loaded with protein will increase your energy level and keep you full until dinner.

WHEN IS THE BEST TIME OF DAY TO HAVE A CUP OF CAFFEINATED COFFEE? Early morning or early afternoon. There is much debate about this, but those who say the morning point out that caffeine can stay in your system for as long as eighteen hours and may throw off your body clock and affect your sleep. So if you're vulnerable to the effects of caffeine, have a cup first thing in the morning and hope it wears off by the time you go to bed. Those who argue for the afternoon say a small cup after lunch can jump-start your afternoon and make you more alert during a time when many people feel sleepy. **Tip:** If caffeine disrupts your sleep, drink a cup or two of caffeine-free herbal tea in the afternoon. **This just in:** Recent coffee studies show: 1) Drinking coffee in moderation doesn't increase the risk of heart disease, hypertension, or pancreatic or kidney cancer, as once thought. What's more, it enhances mood and improves alertness and reaction time, averting an untold number of auto and other accidents. 2) Caffeine has been found to reduce post-workout soreness by as much as 48 percent, so drink some before you work out—and plenty of water during and after. 3) Those who drink caffeinated coffee had a 30 percent lower risk of Parkinson's disease, and heavy coffee drinkers—four to six cups a day—had a 28 percent lower risk of type 2 diabetes. 4) Coffee drinkers tend to gain more weight than those who don't drink it.

WHEN IS THE BEST TIME OF DAY TO HAVE A CUP OF COFFEE IF YOU *DO* WANT YOUR SLEEP DISRUPTED? Late night and early morning hours. That's when fatal vehicle crashes spike. **FYI:** A study by French scientists found that coffee perks up nearly all drivers, regardless of age, weight, sex, or ethnicity. Another study found that just smelling fresh-brewed coffee was enough to perk up a group of lab rats exposed to the aroma.

WHEN IS THE BEST TIME TO DEFROST YOUR FREEZER? When the ice buildup reaches one-quarter-inch deep. You'll waste energy if you do it more or less often.

WHEN IS THE BEST TIME OF YEAR TO GET A TATTOO? Winter. Exposure to the sun—and sweat—can slow healing that needs to occur after you get a tattoo, and you're more likely to avoid that exposure when you're wearing sweaters, coats, and other winter clothes.

Also, lots of people get tattoos during the spring and summer because they don't want to wait to show them off, so lines at tattoo parlors are shorter during the winter.

WHEN IS THE BEST TIME OF DAY TO GET A HAIRCUT? Nine o'clock, or whenever your barber shop or salon opens. At that time, no latecomers will have thrown off the schedule. Many stylists say this is the time of day they are most enthusiastic about their jobs and are experiencing the least stress, largely because they have yet to be exposed to difficult clients. **Tips:** 1) On Saturdays, don't walk in without an appointment; some salons schedule bridal parties first thing in the morning. 2) Ask your stylist his or her favorite time to cut hair and schedule your appointments then.

WHEN IS THE BEST TIME TO THROW OUT YOUR MAKEUP AFTER USING IT? After six months. Your skin typically changes shades about every six months, so that's a good rule of thumb. But also pay attention to how your makeup looks and smells. If you think you should throw it out, go ahead and do it. Here are some more specific recommendations:

FOUNDATION: After six to eight months—eight months if you use a pump foundation and aren't dabbing your fingers in it every day.

LIPSTICK, LIP GLOSS, AND LIP LINER: After two years.

LIQUID EYELINER: After six months, unless it gets clumpy and dry or your eyes get irritated.

MASCARA: After three months. Most manufacturers say it remains fresh that long.

NAIL POLISH: After two years, unless it comes in contact with a fungal infection before then.

PENCIL EYELINER: After one or two years if it's stored properly and sharpened regularly.

POWDER FACE MAKEUP: After one year.

WHEN IS THE BEST TIME TO TRIM YOUR NAILS? After you've soaked them in a warm bath for about fifteen minutes. Your nails are softer and easier to trim then. Same goes for filing down corns and calluses. **Tip:** Soaking your hands and feet in hot water, as so many bathtub lovers do, will dry out your skin.

WHEN IS THE BEST TIME TO GET OUT OF THE SHOWER? Five minutes after you get in. You'll use only about twelve gallons of water with a low-flow showerhead. A fifteen-minute shower uses nearly forty gallons of water, and most people use thirty to thirty-five gallons when they take a bath. **Water-saving tip:** Turn the water off while you're soaping your body or lathering your hair and you'll use only about five gallons of water.

WHEN IS THE BEST TIME TO REPLACE YOUR TOILET FLAPPER? Once a year. Flappers, those rubber devices that keep water from leaking from the toilet tank into the toilet bowl, break down faster than most manufacturers lead you to believe. And when they do, you can have a subtle leak that you may not notice for weeks or months. **Did you know?** A severe toilet leak can waste as much as 500 gallons of water per day. **Tip:** Plumbers recommend putting a dye tablet in your tank. If the color of the water in your toilet bowl changes, you have a leak.

WHEN IS THE BEST TIME OF DAY TO WATER YOUR LAWN? Early morning. Watering at night often leads to fungus and mold problems because the lawn becomes saturated at a time when very little evaporation can occur. Watering during the heat of the day is wasteful because too much evaporation occurs. **FYI:** About 40 percent of those who participated in a recent survey water at the wrong time, and 47 percent water too often. A good watering—soaking at least one inch below the roots—once a week usually is enough for an established lawn.

WHEN IS THE BEST MONTH OF THE YEAR TO HAVE A TREE CUT DOWN? January or February—take your pick. Post-Christmas credit card bills arrive by then, and who wants to write a check to a tree trimming company unless a big limb is leaning on your roof? As a result, tree companies are hungry for business, and prices are lower, especially if you let the businesses know they have competition for the work. An added benefit to the winter: no leaves to rake afterward.

WHEN IS THE BEST TIME TO MULCH YOUR LEAVES IF YOU USE A MOWER THAT CAN MULCH THEM? When they're less than an inch deep on your lawn. Too many leaves means too much mulch, which will block the sun and rain from going where they need to go.

WHEN IS THE BEST TIME TO PICK A FLOWER? Right before it blooms. Cut it and put it in water, and chances are you'll get to see it open and enjoy it for many days afterward. Roses might be the exception: They may not open if you cut them before they bloom.

WHEN IS THE BEST TIME TO BUY AND PLANT BUSHES AND TREES? The fall. Nurseries and home stores often sell plants at their lowest prices of the year in the fall. And with the heat of the summer gone, plants have time to establish their roots before winter brings severe weather. Plants, like people, don't tend to multitask well. In the fall, they begin establishing their root systems, when they don't have to worry about growing leaves and flowers. So planting in the fall will allow them to concentrate on their roots, giving them a better chance to survive. **Tips from nurserymen:** 1) Make sure new plants get at least an inch of water per week through November. 2) Spread a layer of mulch around plants to help keep the ground warmer so they can have more time to grow in the fall. 3) Despite this, some plants do better if planted in the spring. Here's a short list: rhododendrons, yew, oaks, hornbeams, magnolias, larch, sweet gum, gingko, and hemlock.

WHEN IS THE BEST TIME TO PLANT VEGETABLES? It depends on where you live, but some plants are very tolerant of the cold. Plants considered very tolerant—asparagus, horse-radish, leeks, onions, parsnips, peas, spinach, turnips, and shallots—can be put in the ground as soon as the ground can be worked. Plants that are not as hearty but still considered somewhat cold tolerant—beets, broccoli, cabbage, carrots, cauliflower, celery, collards, lettuce, kale, and endive—can be planted two to four weeks before the first average frost-free date. And frost-sensitive plants—melons, peppers, tomatoes, sweet corn, eggplant, cucumbers, artichokes, and squash—should go in the ground well after the last frost.

WHEN IS THE BEST TIME OF THE YEAR TO PLANT FRUIT TREES? Late autumn or early spring. The climate needs to be mild, or the trees won't survive. **Other tips:** 1) Some fruit trees, including apples, need to be planted near compatible trees so they can pollinate each other, or they won't bear fruit. 2) Buy a one-year-old tree with undamaged branches. Don't worry if the branches are very thin. Prune them and they'll thicken.

WHEN IS THE BEST TIME OF THE YEAR TO KILL DANDELIONS? The fall. A lot of people want to spray dandelions in the spring, soon after they pop out of the ground, but many dandelions are seemingly unaffected by herbicides this time of year. Fall is the best time because that's when they're in a growth cycle that makes them more vulnerable to weed killers. And dandelions usually are not flowering then, so the poison won't harm the birds that eat the plants' seeds. **But:** If you've had a hard frost, it's probably too late to try to kill dandelions with a herbicide—the cold tends to shut down their systems, and they won't respond to poison. And don't try to pull them out of the ground: They have extensive root systems, so even if you think you got the whole root, you probably didn't. **Another opinion:** Some gardeners and horticulturists swear by hitting dandelions twice with weed killer, in June and then again in September. **The best time of day?** The morning. Apply weed killer then to allow the sun to help the herbicide soak into the plant tissue more effectively.

WHEN IS THE BEST TIME OF THE YEAR TO FERTILIZE YOUR LAWN? Warm-weather holidays. There obviously is no connection between the effectiveness of fertilizer and holidays, but horticulturists have found that fertilizers work best when applied in late spring (Memorial Day), early summer (the Fourth of July), and late summer (Labor Day). And some people find it easier to remember to apply fertilizer if they do it on or near those holidays. **Tip:** Fertilize right before it rains. Fertilizer and water make a great one-two punch as long as you don't overwater and wash away the fertilizer.

WHEN IS THE BEST TIME OF THE YEAR TO TRANSPLANT PERENNIALS? It depends. Wait until the fall to transplant perennials that flower in the spring, and transplant fall-flowering perennials in the spring. Plants that flower in the summer can be moved in the spring or the fall. If you transplant them at different times, they still may survive, but they'll experience more stress.

WHEN IS THE BEST TIME OF THE YEAR TO PLANT COOL-SEASON GRASS? Late summer to early fall. Keep in mind that not all types of grasses grow well everywhere, but cool-season grasses, such as bluegrasses, bent grasses, fescues, and rye, grow best in the fall and spring. In September and October, the ground is warm enough for the seeds to germinate, and the young grasses have the entire fall to become established. **The next-best time?** Early spring. Young grass plants have less time to grow strong before hot weather arrives and stresses them, but they often survive.

WHEN IS THE BEST TIME OF THE YEAR TO PLANT WARM-SEASON GRASS? Late spring. Bermuda, buffalo, St. Augustine, and other warm-season grasses do best when planted in late spring, when the weather is still mild. That allows the grasses to get established before the hot weather comes. The down side to warm-season grass is it becomes dormant during cold weather and homeowners have to tolerate brown lawns. If you can't tolerate that, try overseeding your lawn, but not with another warm-season grass seed. Overseeding is exactly what you think it is: Just sow seeds over your existing lawn. A cool-season grass, especially rye, works best, giving you a green lawn in the winter.

WHEN IS THE BEST TIME OF DAY TO APPLY INSECT REPELLENT? Around dusk and dawn. Some mosquitoes bite throughout the day, but dusk and dawn are when mosquitoes are most active. Many of the best insect repellents contain a chemical called DEET. Repellents that contain the most DEET typically work best, and there are two theories on why it works so well. One says it jams odor receptors in the nervous systems of insects, so the bugs can't smell you. The other claims that mosquitoes smell DEET and don't like it so they fly away. **Did you know?** DEET, which the Army developed after World War II soldiers complained about insect bites, is short for N,N-diethyl-m-toluamide. (Say it fast and your friends will think you can actually pronounce it.)

WHEN IS THE BEST TIME OF THE YEAR TO KILL WASPS? The winter. With the exception of the yellowjacket queen wasp, wasps can't survive in the cold, but their eggs can. So although wasp nests may look abandoned in the winter, inside the queen and the eggs are hibernating. In the winter, when the other wasps have died off, douse the nest with wasp poison and then remove it. If you don't want to handle poison, hire an exterminator, who will have access to stronger insecticides than you can buy.

WHEN IS THE BEST TIME OF THE DAY TO DUMPSTER DIVE? Between 6 p.m. and 8 p.m. Early evening is best because apartment dwellers often take their trash to the Dumpster after they eat dinner, and businesses do so at the end of the workday. If they're throwing out any good stuff, that's when they'll do it, and that's when the experienced Dumpster divers will be there waiting. Less experienced hunters and gatherers may feel more comfortable going later, when it's dark, but those who do that may risk losing out on a free treasure. For those of you who are thinking, "I thought this book was all about providing *practical* tips. I've never Dumpster dived, and I don't know anyone else who has"— well, maybe you should consider it. One experienced diver reports never having to buy the following things: envelopes, clothes, houseplants, candles, Christmas decorations, furniture, toiletries, books, magazines, newspapers, inexpensive jewelry, and more, including half his food!

CHAPTER THREE

BON VOYAGE

W hen you plan a vacation, you want to know the best time to be at your destination. Let's face it, not many tourists go to Minneapolis in February or Houston in August. Beyond the obvious, this chapter reveals many travel-related secrets known only to insiders, such as the best time of the day and day of the week to fly, the best time to check into a hotel to get an upgrade, and the best time to buy travel insurance or book a cruise. You'll also find out the best time to visit Niagara Falls, Disney World/Land, Mount Rushmore, and other popular tourist destinations, as well as the best time to go to Toronto, Rome, Sydney, and many of the world's greatest cities.

WHEN IS THE BEST TIME OF THE DAY TO FLY? Noon. Commercial airline pilots will tell you it depends on which airport you're flying out of, but generally noon is the time when you'll avoid airport rush hours, which often coincide with workday rush hours. Weather also factors into this. For example, West Coast travelers know morning fog often delays flights, as do afternoon thunderstorms in the East. "You want to be on the ground by two in the afternoon in the summer," said one pilot who flies east of the Mississippi. **Another view:** According to a few of the people who decide to cancel flights for U.S. airlines, evening is best because carriers usually work hard to get planes where they need to be in the morning for the next day's flight schedule.

WHICH IS THE BEST DAY OF THE WEEK TO FLY? Saturday. The airlines offer fewer flights on Saturdays, and that translates to fewer delays, shorter lines, and less stress and aggravation for you. Air traffic controllers say if you fly on a Saturday, you're more likely to arrive on time, and if that isn't enough to convince you, Saturday is one of the cheapest days of the week to fly, according to a statistical analysis of millions of airfares. (Tuesdays and Wednesdays are also cheap days to fly, while Sunday is one of the most expensive.) **Check this out:** Go to the National Air Traffic Controllers Association Web site, click on "Media Center," and then choose from a list of the nation's twenty-nine largest airports to learn about the best days to fly.

WHICH IS THE BEST MONTH TO FLY TO YOUR SUMMER VACATION DESTINATION? August. During the past five years, more flights arrived on time in August than July. There's no good explanation for it, but that's what the data show.

WHICH IS THE BEST DAY OF THE WEEK TO SHOP FOR AIRLINE TICKETS? Monday or Tuesday. That's when airlines often offer lower fares, and in fact, Tuesday is when most travelers buy tickets. Airlines raise fares later in the week. What about the widespread belief that airlines offer the best deals from 12:01 to 2:00 a.m. on Wednesdays? Some deals may be had at this time, but it turns out that isn't a widespread practice among the airlines. **Shopping tips:** 1)Weekday domestic fares change about three times a day, so sign up for e-mail alerts. 2) When you book your ticket, it's great to find a nonstop flight, but beware of "direct flights." Many of them stop once en route to their final destinations. 3) Before you buy, check out farecast.com, which will predict whether the price of your flight will go up, down, or stay the same during the next week.

WHEN IS THE BEST TIME OF YEAR TO BUY DOMESTIC AIRLINE TICKETS? Early, but not too early. Shop around as early as you want, but airlines start offering the cheapest seats about three months in advance of a flight. Prices tend to rise within sixty days of a flight and then again within thirty days of a flight. If there are any seats left within twenty days, prices often dip then. Airlines want to fill every seat, and last-minute deals are possible to find, but don't count on it. Demand for flights is high, and carriers are more likely to punish procrastinators by hiking ticket prices within a week or two of a flight. **The exception:** When you plan to fly around the holidays, it's a good idea in that case to lock in a price ASAP if it seems reasonable.

WHEN IS THE BEST TIME OF THE YEAR TO GET A GREAT DEAL ON PREMIUM AIRLINE TICKETS TO EUROPE? Around the end-of-the-year holidays. Why then? Business travelers buy many of the first-class and business-class seats to Europe during most of the year, but business travel slows to a crawl between Thanksgiving and early January. The airlines want to fill these seats, so they often sell them at huge discounts, especially for flights departing from cities in the northeast United States. Some of the folks who track this say they've seen first-class and business-class seats that usually sell for $6,000 to $7,000 go for as little as $900 in December. Most of the airlines don't advertise these rates because they don't want to anger their regular business travelers who pay top dollar the rest of the year. Continental Airlines is the exception. After Continental advertises these inexpensive premium seats, most of the other airlines drop prices to try to match its fares. **The next best time?** The summer. Surprised? Demand for the most expensive seats wanes in the summer, when U.S. business travelers who often go to Europe for work decide to vacation elsewhere. Again, the airlines want to fill the seats that business travelers aren't using, so some first-class seats can sell in the summer for about $1,500—the same or even less than the cost of a coach seat to Europe. How can that be? It's all about supply and demand. The demand for coach seats to Europe in the summer is very high, but first-class and business-class ticket sales drop. **Shopping tip:** Regardless of what type of seat you want, buy international seats within sixty to ninety days of flying.

WHEN IS THE BEST TIME TO REDEEM FREQUENT-FLIER MILES? When an airline announces a new route. The airline's customers haven't flown that route before, so there are plenty of seats to fill, and it's less likely the airlines will give you a hard time about using frequent-flier miles. **Rule of thumb #1:** Many airlines have grounded their biggest planes, have reduced flights, and have fewer seats available, so use frequent-flier miles as quickly as you can. **Rule of thumb #2:** Use frequent-flier miles when you can get more than a dollar's worth of airfare for every eighty frequent-flier miles you spend. For example, you typically need 25,000 frequent-flier miles for a domestic round-trip ticket. Buy the ticket if it costs less than $312.50, and use your frequent-flier miles if it costs more than that. For international flights, which typically require 40,000 to 60,000 miles or more, try for at least $2.25 worth of airfare for every hundred miles. So using 60,000 frequent-flier miles for a round-trip flight that costs $1,350 or more would be a good deal for you.

WHEN IS THE BEST TIME TO GET BUMPED FROM AN OVERBOOKED FLIGHT IN ORDER TO RECEIVE A PAYOUT FROM THE AIRLINES? The later, the better. Passengers who check in late—even if they show up at the gate well before boarding—are more likely to be bumped. If you have a seat assignment, let the gate agent know before any announcement that you might volunteer to give up your seat, then start asking lots of questions about what you can get in exchange. **Other tips:** 1) Don't accept a voucher for much less than $400, the maximum for domestic flights as mandated by the U.S. Department of Transportation. 2) Find out whether the vouchers expire or have blackout dates. 3) Insist that the gate agent get you a seat on another flight before you give up your seat.

WHEN IS THE BEST TIME TO SOCIALIZE AFTER A VERY LONG FLIGHT? Right away. Sleep researchers and others have determined that travelers who retreat to their hotel rooms after arriving at their destinations take longer to recover from jet lag than do those who drop their bags at their hotels and leave to explore and meet people.

WHICH IS THE BEST MONTH TO GO ON VACATION TO RELIEVE THE WINTER DOLDRUMS? March. By March, nearly half of all Northerners have experienced some sort of winter-induced blues, and it's also the month in which those with seasonal affective disorder, or SAD, suffer the most. Go somewhere sunny to get some relief. You don't have to go somewhere warm. Hitting the slopes can be just as therapeutic as hitting the beaches, as long as you soak in plenty of sunshine.

WHEN IS THE BEST TIME OF YEAR TO APPLY FOR A PASSPORT? The fall. It's traditionally a slow time for applications. With fewer applications coming into the State Department then, it usually takes less time to process them. In January, with the new year upon us, people often begin planning trips and realize they'll need a passport. January is the start of a busy season for passport applications that continues until the end of the summer.

WHEN IS THE BEST TIME TO BUY TRAVEL INSURANCE? Almost never. This coverage often duplicates coverage you already have in homeowners and medical insurance and in credit card policies. What's more, airlines must reimburse you for lost luggage, so you don't need travel insurance for that. **An exception:** Consider emergency medical insurance if your health is bad and you're traveling overseas. Medicare typically won't cover you for overseas health expenses, and your insurance company may not, either. **FYI:** Most insurance experts recommend against buying travel insurance for the reasons mentioned above, but since 9/11, about 30 percent of travelers have bought some form of this insurance— up from 10 percent just before the terrorist attacks.

WHICH IS THE BEST DAY OF THE WEEK TO RENT A CAR? Tuesday or Wednesday. By then many business travelers have their cars, but you'll beat the rush for others, especially by big-city dwellers who wait until Thursday or Friday to rent a car for the weekend. **Money-saving tips:** 1) Always decline when rental car companies ask if you want to upgrade. They sometimes ask when they've run out of compact cars. In those cases, you'll often get an upgrade without paying for one. 2) Don't buy insurance from rental car companies. You probably have coverage on your auto insurance, but if you don't, buy it from your insurance agent, who will sell it to you cheaper than will the rental car companies.

WHEN IS THE BEST TIME OF DAY TO GET A FREE RENTAL CAR UPGRADE? The middle of the day. That's especially true in big cities that are destinations for business travelers. The cars business travelers rent are usually off the lots by the middle of the day, so if you show up then, you may get a nicer car than the one you reserved. Keep in mind that with the rising price of gas, you may not want an upgrade if that means a Ford Expedition rather than a Ford Escort.

WHICH IS THE BEST DAY OF THE WEEK TO GET A FREE HOTEL UPGRADE? Sunday or Monday. Those are usually the slowest days of the week, when you're more likely to get an upgrade because more rooms are vacant. It also helps when your Sunday–Monday stay occurs during "low season" wherever you happen to be, such as August in Dallas or January in Minneapolis. **Tips:** 1) Reserve a room directly with the hotel to save it from having to pay fees to travel agents or Internet travel companies. The hotel sometimes will reward you with an upgrade. 2) Book a midpriced room. Don't expect to get an upgrade to the penthouse suite if you're paying $49 a night for a room. 3) Upgrades mean different things to different people, so ask for what you want. Do you want to stay in a suite or do you want a bigger bathroom or a better view? 4) Be nice to the person who checks you into the hotel, and then be patient while he or she works to fulfill your request.

WHEN IS THE BEST TIME OF THE DAY TO GET A HOTEL UPGRADE? The evening. And as late as possible. By then, hotel staffers know how many rooms—and which rooms—will not be filled that night, so you'll have a better chance of getting a great room for a standard price. Those who check in around midnight have a better chance of sleeping in the penthouse suite if someone else hasn't already paid for it. **The exception:** Hotels that cater to business travelers often save the best rooms for their return customers, many of whom also check in at night.

WHEN IS THE BEST TIME TO BUY AN AMTRAK TICKET? ASAP. You can book a train trip eleven months in advance, and if you do so, you're bound to get the best deals. You'll pay the highest fares if you travel around holidays and if you need to start your trip in the morning and end it in the afternoons—rush-hour traffic. **Tip:** Check Amtrak's Web site to see how often the route you want to take is on time. The range is anywhere from 2 percent to nearly 90 percent.

WHICH IS THE BEST MONTH TO BOOK A CRUISE? April or November. That's when many cruise lines move their ships halfway around the globe for route changes. Repositioning these ships isn't cheap, and the cruise lines like to have paying customers on board for these so-called repo cruises. The ships typically have plenty of cabins available, so avoid the temptation to book these cruises several months in advance. Cruise lines will offer good deals—sometimes discounting fares by as much as 50 percent—to put more people aboard. Even if you don't save as much as that, the cost-per-day fare for one of these long cruises is usually much less than for one- or two-week cruises. Keep in mind that these cruises are long and attract a lot of retirees, so if you're looking to party with twentysomethings, think twice before you book. **Another good time:** Check for good deals in the weeks approaching major holidays, when many people like to be at home and cruise lines have a more difficult time finding passengers. **Money-saving tip:** Book a room on a lower deck. The higher the deck, the more it will cost.

WHEN IS THE BEST TIME OF DAY TO GET THE BEST VIEWS FROM THE TOP OF THE EMPIRE STATE BUILDING? Dusk on a clear winter day. This probably is debatable, but here's why one tour guide picks this time: "The sunsets here are every color of the rainbow," she said. "During the cooler months, before you blink, it's dark—and the whole city lights up like someone threw a switch." Not everyone recommends being up there in winter, but everyone says clear skies are the key. If you get that, you can see as far as eighty miles in each direction.

WHEN IS THE BEST TIME OF DAY TO AVOID LINES AT THE EMPIRE STATE BUILDING? Technically, the best time to avoid long lines are foggy and rainy winter days when 1) You'll freeze up on the observation deck; 2) you won't see much of anything; and 3) you'll feel like a chump for throwing away your hard-earned money on a ticket. (The nicest cashiers will try to talk you out of buying a ticket on days like those.) Realistically, the best times are when the building opens (8 a.m.) and when the last elevator ascends to the observation deck (1:15 a.m.). This is before and after the vast majority of New York's other tourist attractions open and close, so why not do it then if you're up and you can't do much of anything else touristy?

WHICH IS THE BEST DAY OF THE YEAR TO GET MARRIED AT THE EMPIRE STATE BUILDING? Valentine's Day. February 14 also happens to be the *only* day of the year it's permitted. But don't think you can just put on a tux or a white dress and drag your sweetheart and a justice of the peace up there. You must apply in writing and then be lucky enough to be picked. **The next best thing?** Propose marriage there. The observation deck on this 1,454-foot building is one of the most popular places in the city to *propose* to your sweetheart, though no one knows with any certainty how many times it has happened. And there's no guarantee she'll say yes.

WHEN IS THE BEST TIME OF DAY TO SEE THE STATUE OF LIBERTY? First thing in the morning. That's when the lines are shortest to buy tickets for the ferry boat that takes you there. That boat usually leaves Battery Park at 9 a.m.

WHEN IS THE BEST TIME OF YEAR TO SEE NIAGARA FALLS? October. It's off-season, so fewer tourists are there, and you can get extra value because the fall foliage is bright and beautiful then. The Maid of the Mist and other boats operate until the end of the month, so you can get an up-close view of the falls. Heartier souls swear by the winter, when hotels offer big discounts and tourists are at their annual low, but it's usually bitterly cold and the boats don't run then.

WHICH IS THE BEST MONTH TO VISIT MARTHA'S VINEYARD? September. The crowds diminish after Labor Day, but the water remains warm, thanks to the Gulf Stream, and restaurants and most of the other summer businesses on the island stay open well into October for late-coming tourists. If that weren't enough, rentals drop in price by 25 percent or more after Labor Day.

WHEN IS THE BEST TIME TO SEE FALL FOLIAGE IN NEW ENGLAND AND OTHER EASTERN STATES KNOWN FOR HAVING SPECTACULAR FALL COLORS? It depends entirely on where you want to go and how much rain has fallen in the year, but here's a pretty reliable breakdown by state:

MAINE: Peak time is early October in the north and mid-October in the rest of the state.
MASSACHUSETTS: Peak time in the western part of the state is early to mid-October. It's mid- to late October in eastern Massachusetts.
NEW HAMPSHIRE: Late September is the peak time in the north, early October in the central part of the state, and mid-October in the south.
NEW YORK: Early October is peak time in the northeast. The peak time in central New York is mid-October. Late October is peak time in the western and southern parts.
PENNSYLVANIA (THE POCONOS): Early to mid-October in the north (Wayne County and parts of Pike County) and west (Carbon County) and mid-October in the center (Monroe County and lower Pike County).
VERMONT: Early October is the peak time in northeast Vermont. Most of the rest of the state is at its peak five or six days later. Most leaves are turning brown by October 20.

WHEN IS THE BEST TIME OF YEAR TO GO TO DISNEY WORLD? The fall. Of those who pick the fall, some say September and others, November. If you have school-age children, both choices will require you to yank them out of school for a couple of days. September is peak hurricane season, but it's less hot and humid than in the summer, and crowds are down, as are off-site hotel prices. In November—pre-Thanksgiving only—the weather is cool but pleasant, the crowds are way down, and Christmas decorations are going up. **The next best time?** May. Crowds and hotel prices are moderate, and the weather is warm and pleasant. **And finally:** If you can only go during the summer and your kids don't start school until after Labor Day, late August is your best bet. It will be hot and humid, but many kids are already back to school in mid- and late August, so it's less crowded than any other time during the summer.

WHEN IS THE BEST TIME OF YEAR TO GO TO DISNEYLAND? The fall. The reasons are much the same as for Disney World—the weather is more mild and there are fewer tourists. And in California, there is no threat of fall hurricanes, which have ruined plenty of Florida vacations. **The disadvantages:** There is a greater chance of rain in the fall, and park hours may be shorter.

WHEN IS THE BEST TIME OF THE YEAR TO TRAVEL TO THE FLORIDA KEYS? The summer. It's true that it's hot and humid in the summer in the Keys, but isn't it hot and humid in much of the country then? The people who live in the Keys point out that the summer is the best time of the year to go boating and snorkeling, and you can find a place to rent for $750 a week, compared to $1,500 or more from December through March. Although it's warmer in the Keys than in much of the rest of the country, during the winter it can still be too cool to do much outdoors.

WHEN IS THE BEST TIME OF DAY TO SEE MOUNT RUSHMORE? Sunrise. Daybreak is particularly flattering for these four former U.S. presidents—George Washington, Thomas

Jefferson, Abraham Lincoln, and Theodore Roosevelt—who, unlike most of the rest of us, look best first thing in the morning thanks to the morning sun. Also, relatively few people bother to get out of bed to see Rushmore at this time, so you won't have to fight the crowds. **A tip:** After you take in this view up close, eat breakfast at the park's Buffalo Dining Room, which offers wonderful views from a distance. While you're eating, you'll get to watch from afar as the crowds begin to jockey for position—and you can feel good that you beat them to the attraction.

WHEN IS THE BEST TIME OF YEAR TO SEE MOUNT RUSHMORE? Early fall. If you go then, you'll miss the brutal cold of winter, the occasional spring snowstorms, and the throngs of summer tourists. More than half of the 2.8 million annual visitors go to Rushmore in the summer. However, if you don't mind the crowds, the summer weather usually is great near the Black Hills—lots of sun, low humidity, and little rain.

WHEN IS THE BEST TIME OF DAY TO VISIT THE GRAND CANYON? Sunrise and sunset. That's when landscape photographers love to be there—a time, they say, when this breathtaking place receives soft light and becomes even more spectacular. It's also when fewer day-trippers will be there.

WHICH IS THE BEST DAY OF THE WEEK TO VISIT THE GRAND CANYON? Wednesday. In the summer, when the crowds are huge, there may not be a best day, at least not on the popular South Rim, where as many as 90 percent of all tourists go. But during the rest of the year, Wednesdays usually are less crowded. Why? Many people go to the Grand Canyon for long weekends, and by Wednesday they've either gone home or they haven't yet arrived.

WHEN IS THE BEST TIME OF THE YEAR TO VISIT THE GRAND CANYON? The spring or the fall. Not the summer, which is high tourist season, and when temperatures in the canyon can reach 120 degrees. (But it's dry heat. Yeah, right.) Keep in mind that the more remote North Rim, which offers incredible views and more privacy, is closed from late October to March, but the South Rim is open year round. **FYI:** Pleasant weather in the spring or fall can quickly turn unpleasant, so keep that in mind if you're planning an overnight hike.

WHICH IS THE BEST MONTH TO GO TO YOSEMITE AND YELLOWSTONE NATIONAL PARKS? May. Temperatures range from the low 40s to the low 70s then, and rain is unlikely. The snow is melting in the mountains, the waterfalls are roaring, and mosquitoes are nowhere to be seen. Wildflowers are out of the ground and trees are blooming. Hiking trails are accessible below 7,000 feet, and during most years the snow is cleared in May so that the main roads are open by Memorial Day. June is also a good month to go, and temperatures can reach into the low 80s then, but by the middle of the month the waterfalls are tuckering out, the hordes of tourists have arrived, and the mosquitoes can cause you to make up new swear words.

WHEN IS THE BEST MONTH TO SAVE MONEY IN LAS VEGAS? January, February, July, or August. Although some would argue that Vegas is for blowing money, not saving it, airfare and hotel prices tend to drop after the busy winter holiday season and during the heat of the summer. Airlines looking to fill planes sometimes offer deals to fly to Vegas during these months. In recent years, August has been especially reasonable.

WHICH IS THE BEST MONTH TO VISIT BERMUDA? May. When most people think of Bermuda, they think of a tropical island, but Bermuda is 1,000 miles *north* of the Caribbean. Its high tourist season is very different from the Caribbean islands' busy season. May is when the best weather starts—warm but not yet humid—and when ocean temps have climbed into the 70s. It's also still possible to find decent hotel deals before the summer season starts. **Another view:** Some swear by October, when the weather is similar to May and the ocean is warmer. But keep in mind that's hurricane season, and despite that, good hotel prices are harder to find then. **The worst time?** The winter. Sure, it's cheaper to travel there then, but it's cold and windy, and there isn't much to do.

WHICH IS THE BEST MONTH TO GO TO THE BAHAMAS? November. December through February is peak tourist season. March and April can be rainy and cool, the summer is too hot for some, and hurricanes are still very real possibilities in September and October. November is still officially hurricane season, but the weather is usually great, with high temperatures in the low 80s and not much rain—or many tourists. **The next best month?** May. You'll find warm weather, but it's rainier, and it's a bit harder to find good deals on hotels.

WHEN IS THE BEST MONTH TO GO TO JAMAICA? January. Sure, you can go in the off-season— May through November—and spend less money, but Jamaica is more fun when you've just escaped a blizzard in Boston, Chicago, or Denver. And January is more likely to be warm there than it is in the Bahamas. Most families that go to Jamaica for Christmas break leave not long after New Year's, and the country's tourist industry is very eager to attract visitors before the busy season, which begins around Presidents' Day and lasts until spring break in April. Many resorts and hotels offer discounts of as much as 50 percent to fill rooms in January. And if you need yet another reason to go, January is typically very sunny, unlike the rainy months of May, June, October, and November. **The next best month?** April. Airlines and hotels often offer good deals in April, but you may want to wait until after spring break. Or not.

WHICH IS THE BEST MONTH TO VISIT PUERTO RICO? May. The peak tourist season starts in December and ends in April, not coincidentally the coldest months of the year in the continental United States and Canada. High temperatures in Puerto Rico barely vary, ranging from 80 degrees in January to 86 degrees in September, but the summer months can be humid and rainy, and hurricanes can ruin Puerto Rican vacations in September and October. That leaves May, when crowds are smaller and many resorts slash their rates to attract tourists.

WHEN IS THE BEST TIME TO VISIT CANCUN? Mid-April to mid-May. This is after spring break and before the busy summer season, so you'll avoid the biggest crowds. Because it's technically off-season, you can get good deals at many of the all-inclusive resorts. And if that weren't enough, the weather is good—warm and dry but not yet unbearably hot and humid.

WHEN IS THE BEST TIME TO VISIT TORONTO? Late September to mid-October. The weather in Canada's largest city and financial capital ranges from warm to brisk in early autumn, but you won't have to worry about heat and humidity or much rain. Also, the trees in the city's parks are beginning to morph into their fall colors, and there are fewer tourists around. It's still not cheap to fly to Toronto in the fall, but there aren't many good airfare deals to be had until January and February, when it can be brutally cold. **Travel tip:** In many cities, Labor Day marks the unofficial end of summer as well as the lowering of prices at hotels and tourist attractions, but that's not true of Toronto. Beginning on the Thursday after Labor Day and lasting ten days, the Toronto International Film Festival attracts tens of thousands of people to view between 300 and 400 films at about two dozen theaters. Cheap flights and downtown hotel rooms are not easy to find then.

WHEN IS THE BEST TIME TO VISIT MONTREAL? The summer. Summers can be hot and humid in Montreal, but only by Canadian standards, so don't let occasional sultry nights keep you away from the historic part of the city and other attractions. The city—the second largest in Canada—has year-round festivals, but the biggest ones are in June, July, and August, and the whole city can seem like one big party then. **Money-saving tip:** Airfare and hotel rates typically are higher in the summer in Canada, Montreal included, but you usually can save on your hotel bill by visiting Montreal during the week.

WHEN IS THE BEST TIME TO VISIT VANCOUVER? The summer. Summer months are usually sunny and warm but not hot in this diverse and cosmopolitan city northwest of Seattle. Although tourists abound then, the city is big enough to absorb them, and Vancouver residents tend to coexist well with them. The city's beaches are a big draw, as is Stanley Park, which has about 500,000 trees on 1,000 acres and annually attracts as many as eight million people, who walk the park's 5.5-mile-long seawall. **The worst time?** Vancouver has the most mild weather you'll find in Canada—it's often compared with southern England—but it's damp and dark and some would say downright gloomy in the winter, not that that stops skiers from flocking to the nearby Whistler resort. While nonskiers tend to stay away from Vancouver in the winter, that won't be the case in 2010, when the city hosts the twenty-first Winter Olympics.

WHEN IS THE BEST TIME TO VISIT NOVA SCOTIA? The first half of October. Most of the tourists, especially those with school-aged children, are long gone by then, and hotels are typically cheaper. And although many of this rugged Canadian province's most popular festivals are in July, August, and September, there's almost as much to do in the fall as in the summer, including whale watching, canoeing, kayaking, hiking, and sailing. Of course, one thing you can't do in the summer is take in the gorgeous fall colors, which attract admirers from as far away as California and Europe. **The worst time?** Even Nova Scotian tourism officials suggest staying away in January, February, and March, when severe weather can make sightseeing and traveling very difficult.

WHEN IS THE BEST TIME TO VISIT LONDON? Spring if you're on a budget, summer if you're not. The arguments for summer are you'll experience the best, sunniest weather of the year. Tourist attractions, such as Buckingham Palace and the House of Parliament, are open to tourists, and there are excellent summer festivals, such as the City of London Festival, the Trafalgar Square Festival, and the Coin Street Festival. Those who prefer spring brag about how much money they save to get there and how short the lines are at tourist traps during "low season." And spring comes early to London, so the weather, while definitely cooler and rainier than in the summer, isn't bad.

WHEN IS THE BEST TIME TO VISIT PARIS? September and early October. The weather is pleasant and Parisians are returning to the city, replacing the summer tourists and bringing with them new energy. Airfares and hotel rates take a dip starting in September, but there still are plenty of outdoor events. Wait much longer than mid-October, though, and risk experiencing cold, dark days and the wrath of Parisians, who are infamous for exhibiting seasonal affective disorder symptoms starting in the late fall.

WHEN IS THE BEST TIME AND DAY TO SEE THE *MONA LISA*? At 9 a.m., Sunday. One of the biggest complaints heard about the Louvre is the long line to see da Vinci's masterpiece. Get there as soon as the museum opens on Sunday morning, when Parisians and tourists are more likely to be sleeping late. Chances are there will still be a line, but it will be shorter than just about any other time you go. **Money-saving tip:** Go on the first Sunday of the month, when it costs nothing to tour the Louvre. **FYI:** While some art enthusiasts adore this painting, many who haven't seen it before are disappointed by its size (only thirty-one by twenty-one inches), by the glare from the glass that protects it from vandals, and by aggressive onlookers who will trample small children to get a good view.

WHICH IS THE BEST MONTH TO VISIT ROME? April. The weather can be a bit cool then, but usually it's pleasant, and there are fewer tourists. And you can get good deals on airfare and hotel rooms in April. **The worst month?** August. The city is hot and sticky and pricey, and tourists outnumber Romans, many of whom flee to the coasts or the mountains for much of the month.

WHICH IS THE BEST MONTH TO VISIT MADRID? May. The weather is pleasant and mostly dry then, and the middle of May is time for the city's most important fiesta of the year, the Fiesta de San Isidro, Madrid's patron saint. This festival features a wide array of events, such as concerts, dances, and bullfights. **Money-saving tip:** Like most of the rest of Europe, March is a good month to save money on airfare and hotel rates as long as you don't mind packing a few sweaters.

WHEN IS THE BEST TIME OF THE YEAR TO VISIT MOSCOW? May and June. This is a time of festivals, carnivals, and concerts, and Muscovites are generally in good spirits, partly because of the pleasant weather. July and August tend to be hot and humid, and the city is crowded with tourists then. **How about St. Petersburg?** June and July. The weather is cooler and drier in these months, there are plenty of festivals, and everyone should experience St. Petersburg's "white nights." These are brightest from June 11 to July 2, when it's daylight twenty-four hours a day. You'll have more time to see the city with arguably the most spectacular architecture in all of Europe. And that's saying something.

WHEN IS THE BEST TIME TO VISIT THE PYRAMIDS OF GIZA? January and February. Fewer Western tourists are there then, and the climate is mild, with high temperatures in the mid-60s. This is the last surviving Wonder of the Ancient World, and it consists of three pyramids—burial places for three Egyptian kings—plus the Great Sphinx, the "Father of Terror," which guards the pyramids. It is believed that about 100,000 men—skilled crafts-man as well as laborers—built the pyramids. Tourists say the best time to go is between 8 a.m. and noon. **Extra tip:** If you want to go inside the pyramids, you'll need to buy tickets. Only 300 a day are sold, and the best times to buy them are either 8 a.m., when they start selling the first 150, and 1 p.m., when they start selling the other 150.

WHICH IS THE BEST MONTH TO CLIMB MOUNT KILIMANJARO? January, February, August, or September. At 19,341 feet, Kilimanjaro is not terribly difficult to climb, unlike Everest and many of the world's tallest mountains. January, February, August, and September are the months when the weather in this part of Tanzania is mildest and climbing is saf-est. Even so, you can't go without a guide, and you'll want to be fit because it takes about a week to reach the summit, Uhuru Peak, the highest point in Africa.

WHEN'S THE BEST TIME TO GO ON SAFARI IN AFRICA? June, July, and August. The winter months—June, July, and August are winter in the Southern Hemisphere—tend to be dry, and that's when wildlife seek out lakes and rivers. You'll have a better chance to get good photos if more animals are crowded together in one place, around pools and lakes. This is the time when the wildebeest migration starts in Kenya and Tanzania, offering views of hundreds of thousands of these animals as well as zebras and the so-called Big Five—lions, rhinos, elephants, leopards, and cape buffalo—moving through the Masai Mara National Reserve in Kenya and the Serengeti in Tanzania and Kenya. These same months are great times to go to national parks in Zimbabwe, South Africa, and Botswana, but be aware that the park roads in Botswana tend to be inaccessible, forcing tourists to rent small planes to see the herds. **Money-saving tip:** Botswana's national parks are beautiful, so if you have your heart set on seeing all that this country has to offer, try May and October when you can find better deals.

Although winter in Africa is the best time to go on safari, the truth is you can go on a safari during any month in Africa. Here's a rundown by month of the prime places:

JANUARY: January, like June, July, and August, is a fairly dry time in Kenya, Tanzania, and Uganda, and so large numbers of animals will hang out by pools. Watch for wildebeest, zebra, and gnu in Tanzania's northern parks.

FEBRUARY: In Tanzania, most wildebeest are born in February in northern parks. Another good reason to stay north: You'll avoid the heat and humidity.

MARCH: East Africa—Kenya, Tanzania, and Uganda—offer good sights in March because it's still fairly dry, and animals congregate by pools.

APRIL: The rainy season starts in East Africa in April, and that means not only that grasses and bush can block your view of the animals, but that some roads get washed out as well. That makes April the best month to find good deals on safaris, especially in Tanzania, where you'll see fewer animals but beautiful landscapes.

MAY THROUGH SEPTEMBER: Zambia is the place to be in May, and the rest of southern Africa is good as the dry season there begins and animals begin congregating in large numbers at pools to quench their thirst.

OCTOBER: Zimbabwe, Kenya, and Tanzania are the best places for a safari in October. The short, rainy season usually hasn't arrived, so herds gather near relatively few watering holes.

NOVEMBER: At Liuwa Plain National Park in Zambia, massive herds of blue wildebeest arrive from Angola, mingling with zebra around watering holes. In northern Tanzania, herds are making their way back to the Serengeti plains.

DECEMBER: Kenya, Tanzania, and Uganda offer tourists dry weather and good viewing.

WHEN IS THE BEST TIME TO GO TO JAPAN? The fall. The fall offers lots of festivals, airfares and hotel rates start dropping in September, and fall foliage is at its best in late October and early November. **Another view:** The spring, when the plum and cherry blossoms are spectacular. But be aware of a common Japanese vacation season called Golden Week, from late April to early May, when many businesses close and the Japanese explore their country. **The worst time?** The summer. It's expensive to get there and stay there, and the weather isn't great. June and July tend to be rainy, and July and August are hot and humid.

WHEN IS THE BEST TIME TO GO TO SYDNEY? December through February. This is summertime in Sydney, a season of festivals, including the January-long Sydney Festival, a celebration of art. These three months are a time of great cultural activity—theater and art exhibit openings—not to mention the best beach weather of the year, with daytime high temperatures in the 80s. But beaches, resorts, and parks are crowded, and hotel fares are higher then, so book early. **How about Melbourne?** January, for some of the same reasons as Sydney. But Melbourne has something that glitzy Sydney does not: the Australian Open tennis championship. Aussies love their tennis, and Melbourne becomes a party town for the two weeks in January when the tournament is happening.

CHAPTER FOUR
ALL WORK AND . . .

Timing is crucial in the workplace, but the proper timing eludes so many workers. The best month to look for a job happens to be when most people assume companies aren't hiring. The best time to drop a bombshell in a meeting is not at the very end, as so often happens. The best time to interview for a job is when most job seekers would call to cancel an interview. The best time to tee off with an important client is not first thing in the morning, when so many businessmen hit the links. The best time to quit and the best time to fire someone happen to be at the same time of day and on the same day of the week. Read on.

WHICH IS THE BEST MONTH TO LOOK FOR A JOB? December. Surprised? While it's true that some companies postpone hiring toward the end of the year to pad their bottom lines before the year ends, many more want to spend their current-year personnel budgets so they won't have to fight so hard to justify asking for the same amount in the future. Also, hiring managers are well aware of their coming-year budgets and want to get a head start on hiring for jobs that start in January. The fact that so many job seekers assume hiring slows to a crawl after Thanksgiving means there is less competition for jobs being filled at the end of the year. **The next best month?** September. Workers sometimes spend summer vacation time interviewing for other jobs, creating openings in the late summer that companies end up filling in early fall. **FYI:** Only about 5 percent of people find jobs by answering help-wanted ads; 23 percent of job seekers use employment agencies, college career offices, or executive search firms; 24 percent contact companies directly; and 48 percent take advantage of personal connections.

WHICH IS THE BEST DAY TO INTERVIEW FOR A JOB? The day after another company has offered you a job. After you receive a job offer, you may be tempted to cancel other scheduled interviews with a company, but that's the last thing you should do. With a job offer sitting on the table, your confidence couldn't be higher, and that will help you make a great impression. That confidence and your positive attitude can be worth a lot of money to you when it comes to negotiating a salary and benefits. If you have another offer in hand, you'll have nothing to lose. Your supreme confidence may cause the hiring manager to offer you a job, but it probably won't cause him to offer you the most the company is willing to pay you. You've got to ask for what you want or else you won't get it, and you can't be afraid to ask for more money. **Another view:** Friday. Many people report being in the best mood and more relaxed at the end of the week, and that can only be a good thing when you're interviewing.

WHEN IS THE BEST TIME OF DAY TO ASK FOR A PAY RAISE? Five o'clock. The end of the workday is often a time when your boss is not rushed and has time to listen. Many supervisors say late afternoon is when they're in the best mood because they know they're going home soon. What's more, your elevated body temperature in the late afternoon usually makes you more alert at that time and perhaps in a better position to make your case. If you work in a newspaper newsroom, a fast-food restaurant, or in another place that's hectic during the late afternoon, avoid that time. Instead, monitor your boss's daily habits to determine the best, most low-key time for him or her.

WHICH IS THE BEST DAY OF THE WEEK TO ASK FOR A PAY RAISE? Thursday or Friday. We're most open to negotiation and compromise then because most of us want to finish our workweek with the least amount of conflict. This feeling at the end of the workweek may be preparation for the weekend, when we spend more time with family and friends, getting along with whom is a high priority. Others point out that Fridays also are the best day to give favorable performance reviews, so if you receive one then, ask for a big raise. **The worst day?** Wednesday. Unpleasantness and surliness tend to peak then, so try to avoid any situation that can lead to conflict. **Tips:** 1) Don't ask for a raise during year-end budget planning, when your company is getting audited or when your boss is distracted by pressing matters. Wait for some good news. 2) Keep a file folder that documents your accomplishments, which you'll need to rattle off to your boss when you make your case for a hefty raise.

WHEN IS THE BEST TIME OF THE DAY TO STRATEGIZE, BRAINSTORM, OR SOLVE PROBLEMS? Late morning. This is when your body temperature rises, and when that happens, you're more alert and your brain can process information better. The worst time? The afternoon. In the early afternoon, there's a dip in body temperature that causes sleepiness, and it's also when your circadian rhythms—the pattern of physical and mental changes we repeat every 24 hours—trigger sleepiness. Late afternoon isn't a good time to solve problems at work, either, because workers can become distracted as they think more about going home than about working. **Tips for managers:** 1) Make sure that if you call a brainstorming meeting, you genuinely want input and are not just looking for validation of decisions you've already made. 2) Look for opportunities for spontaneous brainstorming, which can create a sense of urgency that brings out the best in some workers.

WHEN IS THE BEST TIME OF DAY TO MAKE A PRESENTATION? Mid-morning. You're fairly alert by then, as is your audience, and your voice is rested. **The worst time?** The afternoon, for the same reasons that it's a bad time to strategize and brainstorm. Public speakers dread addressing audiences in the early afternoon. They say it's the hardest time of the day to keep their attention.

WHICH IS THE BEST DAY OF THE WEEK TO COMPLAIN TO YOUR BOSS? Thursday or Friday. Mondays are often hectic meeting days, when you're less likely to have your boss's ear. Tuesdays are widely considered the most productive day of the workweek, a day when work takes priority over everything else. Wednesdays tend to be the surliest day of the week, when tensions are highest and you want to avoid conflict. Thursdays or Fridays are days when we're most open to compromise because we're hoping to finish our workweek with the least amount of conflict. They are good days to ask for favors and convince a supervisor to see your side of a situation.

WHEN IS THE BEST TIME TO TELL AN EMPLOYER ABOUT A DISABILITY? When the disability causes you to need help. If the disability is not affecting your work, it's not relevant. If it's causing work-related problems, disclose it then, but do so in a positive way, and be reasonable if you make a request. For example, say something like: "I would be even more productive if I worked from home a couple of days a week because I have a medical condition that . . ." **Another view:** Disclose it before you get the job, but only after you've convinced your interviewers you have the skills and ability to do a good job. Managers will respect the fact that you disclosed your disability before you landed the job.

WHEN IS THE BEST TIME TO START A BUSINESS? When you have the time to devote to it. Although many entrepreneurs have started a business when they're working another job, you have the best shot at success if you give yourself the time to focus on it. And you have to be ready and willing to face new challenges, so if you're experiencing a lot of stress—a divorce, a move, a death in the family—wait until you've gotten through the worst of it.

WHICH IS THE BEST DAY OF THE WEEK TO SHUT DOWN YOUR FIRM FOR A COMPANY-WIDE MEETING? Friday. A survey of Canadian executives who are polled every few years always comes to the same conclusion: Friday is the least productive day of the workweek and a great day to shut things down. The theory is that productivity wanes as the weekend nears, and workers need more supervision to get their work done on Thursdays and Fridays. **The worst day?** Tuesdays. The latest survey found that 54 percent of the executives said their employees are most productive on Tuesdays, followed by Mondays (21 percent), and Wednesdays (15 percent), though many supervisors who didn't participate in this survey consider Wednesdays more productive than Mondays. Another vote for Tuesdays comes from a behavioral psychologist who says workers tend to be demanding and disagreeable on Tuesday, but that can increase productivity. She says, "Dominant behaviors are frequently about getting things done—setting goals, organizing work, assigning responsibilities."

WHEN IS THE BEST TIME OF THE DAY TO HOLD A MEETING? At an odd time. That is, schedule a meeting for 10:10 a.m. rather than at 10 a.m. or at 3:35 p.m. rather than at 3:30

p.m. Why? You'll get employees' attention. They're more likely to remember a meeting scheduled for 10:10 a.m., and many people will make more of an effort to arrive on time out of curiosity, if for no other reason. Meetings that start late waste time and money, so some managers are trying this, and they say it works. **Meeting tips for managers:** 1) Start on time—no matter what. If you don't, you'll send the message that it's okay to be late, and you'll end up punishing employees who are prompt. 2) Close the door when the meeting begins. That will draw more attention to those who are tardy. Some managers send an even stronger message by locking doors after a meeting begins. 3) Print a meeting agenda and make sure the most important matters are discussed first. If you don't, some will think they can skip the beginning of the meeting without missing much of importance. **Did you know?** Many managers report spending as much as three-fourths of their workdays in meetings. Most of that time, they say, is unproductive.

WHEN IS THE BEST TIME TO DROP A BOMBSHELL DURING A MEETING, SPEECH, OR PRESENTATION?

Within the first ten minutes. By the end of the first ten minutes of most presentations, about 80 percent of the audience has usually checked out mentally. Nobody knows exactly why this happens, but scientists theorize that for a number of reasons, the brain makes a subconscious choice to tune out and focus our attention on matters that seem more pressing. **Tip:** To keep your audience's attention, surprise them every ten minutes with a visual, a sound bite, or an interesting anecdote.

WHEN IS THE BEST TIME TO EXPECT GREATNESS FROM AN EMPLOYEE?

When they're young. Many people, especially the brightest and most ambitious, do their most groundbreaking work not long after their college years. This is the time of their lives when they're often most passionate about their careers and are willing to work long hours—at relatively low pay—and put their personal lives on hold. When he was twenty-six, while working at the Swiss patent office, Albert Einstein published four groundbreaking papers, one of which led to his theory of relativity. Industrialist Andrew Carnegie became rich in his twenties. By thirty, Henry Ford was well on his way to revolutionizing the automobile industry. Thomas Edison patented his first invention, the electric vote recorder, when he was twenty-two, and by thirty he had invented the phonograph. Nobel Prize–winning research is often done by scientists and economists during the first ten years of their careers and acknowledged decades later. And many of the Information Age's biggest names, such as Steve Jobs (Apple), Bill Gates (Microsoft), Larry Page and Sergey Brin (Google), and Jerry Yang and David Filo (Yahoo!), started their hugely influential companies while they were still in college.

WHEN IS THE BEST TIME OF DAY TO TEE OFF WITH A CLIENT? Late afternoon. Assuming it doesn't get dark early, this is a good time to show off your golf skills because hand-eye coordination reaches optimal levels then. Moods also tend to be better as the end of the workday approaches. And starting a golf game in the late afternoon means you and your client can go from the golf course to the club restaurant and bar to talk business without having to worry about rushing back to work. So even if there's enough daylight only for nine holes, go for it.

WHICH IS THE BEST MONTH FOR WORKERS TO TAKE A VACATION? July or August. Nearly 60 percent of 150 senior executives surveyed at large companies picked one of those two months. August was ranked highest (36 percent), followed by July (21 percent) and December (14 percent), and 10 percent had no preference. At many companies, business slows down during the summer and just before the end of the calendar year, so fewer workers are needed then, making it a good time to be out of the office.

WHEN IS THE BEST TIME TO TAKE YOUR WORK CELL PHONE WITH YOU ON VACATION? Never. A study of 800 college professors in the United States, New Zealand, and Israel found that those who brought a work cell phone, BlackBerry, or laptop on vacation with them didn't experience the relief from stress that a vacation is supposed to offer. Your boss may admire you for your dedication to the job, but job stress can lead to burnout, and that hurts productivity. **Strange but true:** Arawak Beach Inn, an oceanfront hotel on the Caribbean island of Anguilla, has offered an "Isolation Vacation" that *requires* guests to turn in their electronic gadgets at check-in and *forbids* them Internet access, phones, and TVs. To make up for it, the hotel offers a private day trip to an uninhabited island with a gourmet picnic lunch, a deep-sea fishing trip, three days of snorkel equipment, and more.

WHEN IS THE BEST TIME TO PREPARE AN EXIT STRATEGY AND START LOOKING FOR ANOTHER JOB? When you're still excited about the one you have. This may seem disloyal to the company paying your salary and providing benefits, but you always need to prepare for the worst. No job will last forever, so make sure you're always ready to move on. **Tips:** 1) Assemble a personal board of career advisors upon whom you can call for job-hunting tips, letters of reference, and practice for interviews. These people can also help you decide whether you should accept a job offer. 2) Sign up with online networking sites, such as LinkedIn.com and Facebook.com. The more extensive your network, the easier you'll find job hunting.

WHEN IS THE BEST TIME AND DAY TO TELL YOUR BOSS YOU'RE QUITTING? Five o'clock, Friday, for the same reason it's the best time to ask for a raise—your boss is usually in a good mood. And if your news changes his mood, it's the end of the workweek, and you both can go home, allowing the news sink in before you return to work on Monday. **Tip:** Don't have this conversation until you are absolutely sure you have another job. Your boss may react by giving you fifteen minutes to find some cardboard boxes and pack up your things.

WHEN IS THE BEST TIME TO ACCEPT A COUNTEROFFER FROM YOUR EMPLOYER? When you're sure the factors that make you want to leave the company will change. If all you want is more money, accepting a big pay raise from your company and turning down an offer from someone else may be the right decision. If you receive a counteroffer from your employer, you can be certain your employer wants to keep you—at least in the short term—so you are negotiating from a strong position. This also may be your best opportunity to ask for better, more flexible hours, more vacation time, more training, and even an office—or a bigger and better one. **Don't forget:** If you receive a counteroffer from your employer, get everything in writing. And speaking of writing, send a thank-you note to the person at the other company who offered you a job. It's a small world, and you never know if you'll end up working there someday.

WHEN IS THE BEST TIME OF DAY TO FIRE SOMEONE? Late afternoon. Chances are, you'll sadden the employee no matter when you do it, but if you do it late in the afternoon, there are two advantages: 1) Fewer people are in the office then, so the situation will be more private and confidential; and 2) you probably won't kill him. Seriously: Heart attacks are more likely to happen in the first three hours after awakening, and 30 percent to 40 percent more likely to occur between 6 a.m. and noon, when blood pressure and heart rate peak, putting stress on arterial walls. The American Heart Association has even weighed in on this, recommending that all firings and layoffs occur after 10:00 a.m.

WHICH IS THE BEST DAY OF THE WEEK TO FIRE SOMEONE? Friday. Some workers need to be fired on the spot, but if businesses can wait, managers make this tough decision on

Fridays, sometimes referred to as "Firingday." They prefer Fridays for three reasons: 1) It gives colleagues the weekend to let the news sink in; 2) it gives managers the opportunity to change locks or clean out offices during the weekend; and 3) it allows the departing worker to earn a full week's pay before being dismissed. **Another view:** Some executives say firing people on Fridays ruins everyone's weekends. These people suggest doing it on Mondays and getting bad news out of the way early in the week.

WHEN IS THE BEST TIME OF DAY TO CALL YOUR FINANCIAL ADVISER? Eight to nine in the morning. Or thirty minutes after he or she gets to work and is able to drink some coffee, read a few e-mails, and review his or her to-do list. This is one of the calmest times of an adviser's day, which usually gets hectic between 9:30 a.m. and 4 p.m., when the stock market is open and when most meetings occur. Don't call after the market closes, by the way, because many advisers use that time to catch up on paperwork before they go home for the day.

WHEN IS THE BEST TIME OF DAY TO CALL YOUR ACCOUNTANT OR LAWYER? Again, 8 a.m. to 9 a.m. Most accountants and lawyers say they prefer to return phone calls the same day they receive them, so if you call early in the workday and leave a message, your chances of speaking to your accountant or lawyer that day increase because he or she has more time to return your call. Calling in the afternoon gives them less time to return your call that day, even if that's their preference. **Tip:** This applies to other professionals, some of whom often won't return calls in the afternoon unless they're urgent.

WHEN IS THE BEST TIME OF YEAR TO CONTACT YOUR ACCOUNTANT? The fall, preferably between October 15 and the end of November. If you call then, your accountant will have plenty of time to help you make tax-saving adjustments before the end of the year. There still may be a few things they can help you with if you call as late as December 31, but they don't advise procrastinating. **The worst times?** Mid-March to mid-April. Don't call just before tax returns are due. Also, the thirteenth and fourteenth of most months are bad because many accountants face various deadlines—tax payments, tax returns, and other paperwork—that fall on the fifteenth of nearly every month.

WHEN IS THE BEST TIME AND DAY TO FIND A SYMPATHETIC INSURANCE CLAIMS ADJUSTER? Four o'clock, Friday. Sorry to sound like a broken record, but this is a factor that apparently can't be denied: Claims adjusters almost unanimously say they are in a good mood right before the weekend starts. At this time they're more likely to allow, say, someone with a rental car to keep it a few more days. Many adjusters say they've given people breaks late Friday afternoon that they never would have given them on a Monday morning, a Wednesday afternoon, or any other time of the week. **FYI:** Claims adjusters say they're in an especially good mood right before they go on vacation. You won't have any way of knowing when that it is—except that that time is also most likely to be on a Friday afternoon.

WHEN IS THE BEST TIME OF THE DAY AND DAY OF THE WEEK TO REACH 24/7 TECH SUPPORT? Between 6 a.m. and 8 a.m. on weekdays, regardless of what time zone you're in. Some would say there is no good time to call, let alone a best time, but techies report wake-up time as the best time. **FYI:** A 2007 survey of more than 23,000 computer users found that nearly seven out of ten customers were highly satisfied when they hired independent techies, while only about four out of ten were highly satisfied with their computer makers' support staff. Of the latter group, Apple's staff was rated the highest and Compaq's the lowest.

WHEN IS THE BEST TIME OF THE MONTH FOR A BUSINESS TO SIGN A CONTRACT WITH A VENDOR?
The end. This is typically when vendors—office cleaners, uniform companies, office supply distributers, computer techies, and others—are trying to meet monthly revenue goals and are more likely to offer good deals to attract new customers. **The worst time?** The beginning of the month. For the same reason, vendors feel as if they're in the driver's seat when they have most of the month left to hit their targets.

WHEN IS THE BEST TIME TO MAKE COLD CALLS? Early afternoon if you're in the East. Many advocates of cold-calling recommend blocking off the same hour every day to increase the likelihood that cold-calling will become a routine part of your workday. Salespeople who call all over the country say the afternoon in the East is best because you can reach people from coast to coast while they're at work. **A second opinion:** The best time to cold-call is whenever you're in a good mood. **Tips:** 1) Research whom you should call before you call. 2) Have a good script, but don't read from it. 3) Be polite. 4) Always ask for a specific appointment. 5) Don't give up. Did you know that 80 percent of new sales are made after the fifth contact, but most salesmen give up after the second call?

WHEN IS THE BEST TIME OF DAY TO COLD-CALL A BIG SHOT? Between 7 a.m. and 8:30 a.m. Many top executives—the real decision makers—rose in the company because they work a lot of hours, and many of them get to work early to catch up on paperwork and answer e-mails. So call then, before their secretaries arrive, start answering their phones, and block you from talking with them. Will the executive be angry that you're interrupting him during a time when he hoped to get some work done? Maybe, but it's more likely that he'll be impressed that you also share his work ethic and start work early.

WHEN IS THE BEST TIME TO SEND MASS-MARKET E-MAILS TO MOMS? Between 6 p.m. and 8 p.m. That's when moms are cooking dinner and getting their kids ready for bed. Between 8 p.m. and 10 p.m., when they have time to check their e-mail, yours will be at or near the top of their in-boxes.

WHICH IS THE BEST DAY OF THE WEEK TO SEND A BUSINESS E-MAIL THAT WILL BE READ? Tuesday, Wednesday, or Thursday. One research firm determined that about 62 percent of e-mail is opened between Tuesday and Thursday. As for the time of day, most is opened throughout the day—about 80 percent between 8 a.m. and 8 p.m. (EST). Predictably, most business-oriented customers are more likely to open e-mail during their workday, while others may do so at any time during the day. **Another view:** Another firm did a study of 800 million e-mails at 2,000 companies and concluded that most people open e-mails on Fridays, closely followed by Wednesdays and Thursdays. But most people don't click on embedded links in e-mails on those days. E-mails sent on the weekends received the highest click-through rates—possibly because readers have more time then and receive fewer e-mails—but only 3 percent of all e-mails were sent on Saturdays and Sundays.

WHICH IS THE BEST DAY OF THE WEEK TO RELEASE NEWS THAT YOU WANT JOURNALISTS TO REPORT? Monday. Even in these days of 24/7 news, most reporters still work Monday through Friday, and some aren't great about planning their workweeks in advance. Public relations pros realize this and send press releases on Mondays, a day when many reporters are eager for bits of news to jump-start their workweeks.

WHEN IS THE BEST TIME OF THE DAY AND DAY OF THE WEEK TO RELEASE NEWS THAT YOU WANT JOURNALISTS TO MISS? Friday afternoon. Friday is the most common day for reporters to take off. Which makes it the best day for a company or government agency to release bad news about itself. Companies or agencies often wait until Friday afternoon because that gives reporters less time to thoroughly report the story. What's more, stories released on Fridays are published on Saturdays or broadcast on Friday nights—times when fewer readers are reading and fewer viewers are viewing.

WHICH IS THE BEST DAY OF THE WEEK TO HAVE A MASS MAILING ARRIVE? Monday. This is an answer no one wants to swear by, but here's the logic behind it: The amount of work you have at your job and at home often builds as the week goes on because you don't learn about all of the challenges and problems you'll have in a given week until after the week begins. That means you'll have a bit more free time to do things early in the week, and that includes reading the mail. What's more, mail tends to pile up as the week goes on, and the taller the pile, the less likely it is that anyone will want to dig through it during the week. **Did you know?** Women are more likely than men to read direct mail, according to one study, which found that 85 percent of women ages twenty-five to forty-four read it. In another study, 68 percent of those in Generation X (born between 1965 and 1972) and 73 percent of Generation Y (born between 1977 and 1994) say they've used coupons they received from direct mail. In this age of electronic mail and online deals, 75 percent of these groups rate the snail mail they receive as valuable.

CHAPTER FIVE

GET WELL SOON

Our bodies are incredibly complicated machines that perform specific functions at specific times. Knowing these times helps many doctors know how and when to treat their patients. And it can help you, too. After you read this chapter, you'll know the best time to do a cardio workout, brush your teeth, apply sunscreen, have your eyes dilated, eat, stop eating, get a flu shot, take asthma medication and vitamins, and much more.

WHEN IS THE BEST TIME OF DAY TO SEE YOUR DOCTOR? Nine in the morning. You won't have to wait as long then because no one has scheduled an appointment before you, except for walk-in patients with pressing needs. And if you're in the hospital and a doctor finds that you need some sort of treatment early in the day, it's almost a guarantee that you'll receive the treatment that day. Hospital patients seen by doctors in the afternoon or at night sometimes have to wait until the next morning to receive treatment, unless they absolutely have to have it that day. **The next best time?** One o'clock in the afternoon. If your doctor takes a lunch break, as most do, this is a good time because patients with late-morning appointments are long gone by 1:00 p.m. So when you show up then, there's no one with an appointment before yours waiting ahead of you.

WHEN IS THE BEST TIME OF DAY TO SEE YOUR DENTIST? One in the afternoon or after 3 p.m. For the same reason 1 p.m. is a good time to see your doctor, it's also a good time to see your dentist: no waiting. Late afternoon is a good time for a biological reason: You can best tolerate pain from cold and other stimuli—for example, pokes from sharp metal instruments—at that time. **The worst times?** Nine-thirty and one-thirty. Patients with appointments at 9:30 a.m. and 1:30 p.m. often are kept waiting while hygienists struggle to clean the teeth of patients with 9 a.m. or 1 p.m. appointments who arrived with some breakfast and lunch still in their mouths. **FYI:** Anyone with high blood pressure should stay away from the dentist's office in the morning, when blood pressure peaks. Any stress associated with a visit to the dentist will only aggravate your condition.

WHEN IS THE BEST TIME TO BRUSH YOUR TEETH? About an hour after you eat. Many foods contain acids that soften tooth enamel. After about an hour, the acids drain away, and the enamel hardens again. If you brush while the acids are still around, the combination of brushing and acid can damage the enamel. The acids take their own sweet time to leave your teeth, so rinsing your mouth with water or mouthwash won't help get rid of them sooner. **Did you know?** A recent study of nearly 1,000 people found that people who ate as little as three ounces of yogurt a day suffered from less gum disease than those who ate less than that. The researchers concluded that yogurt can neutralize the bacteria that lead to tooth loss and receding gums. **Tip:** Replace your toothbrush at least every three months—or sooner if the bristles are spread out. An old toothbrush is more likely to contain bacteria that go from the brush to your mouth.

WHEN IS THE BEST TIME TO TAKE A PREGNANCY TEST? After your period is between a week and two weeks late. The time it takes for a fertilized egg to implant in the uterus wall can vary, but a pregnancy test will usually detect pregnancy eight to twelve days after ovulation. If you think you're pregnant and you believe you ovulated more than eight days ago, it's a good time to take a pregnancy test. Keep in mind that the accuracy of home tests varies, so always verify results with your doctor as soon as possible.

WHICH IS THE BEST DAY OF THE WEEK TO GET A VASECTOMY? Friday. Urologists give two reasons for this: 1) Many patients who undergo this procedure are embarrassed to talk about it, so if they have it done on a Friday, they can heal during the weekend and return to work on Monday and without anyone the wiser. 2) One of the most important things you can do after getting a vasectomy is nothing. After the surgery, you need to lie on the couch for forty-eight hours with an ice pack between your legs. And if you have to do that, you might as well do it on the weekend, when it's more likely that your wife and kids will be around to bring you books and magazines and snacks.

WHEN IS THE BEST TIME TO WEAN A BABY? Twelve months or more after birth. The American Academy of Pediatrics recommends breast-feeding exclusively for the first six months, then gradually introducing solid foods while continuing to breast-feed for at least an additional six months. Most babies won't reject the breast before their first birthdays. The World Health Organization recommends breast-feeding for at least two years, though most American mothers stop breast-feeding well before then. **FYI:** A recent study involving 8,457 mothers in Belarus who participated in an extensive breast-feeding education program had children who at six and a half years old scored significantly higher on vocabulary and verbal IQ tests than did the children of 7,856 mothers who did not participate in the program. The study's lead author attributed that to breast-feeding. Another reason could be that mothers who care enough to seek information about breast-feeding may be educated themselves and may help their children succeed in school.

WHICH IS THE BEST DAY OF THE WEEK TO EXERCISE? Monday. It sets a psychological tone for the rest of the week. People who work out on Monday are more likely to exercise more often throughout the week.

WHEN IS THE BEST TIME TO STRETCH YOUR MUSCLES? Not right before exercise, as many people assume. Many trainers say stretching cold muscles can strain them, so take a brisk, five-minute walk first. In fact, some suggest stretching after your workout when your muscles are warm and more receptive to stretching. It's not a bad idea to stretch a few times a day—late morning, early afternoon, and late afternoon—especially if you have a desk job. **Did you know?** There is growing debate about the benefits of stretching, and dozens of studies disagree on whether stretching helps athletic performance and cuts down on injuries, as is widely assumed.

WHEN IS THE BEST TIME TO DO A CARDIO WORKOUT? Between 5 p.m. and 7 p.m. That's when your lungs use oxygen more efficiently, flexibility peaks, and you're more coordinated, so you're less likely to hurt yourself. Another good reason to do it then: Exercise can relieve stress after your workday. But what about the argument that you should do cardio on an empty stomach, when you're more likely to burn fat? Although some studies suggest there is truth to that, your body won't perform as well if it doesn't have fuel—that is, food. **Tip:** Finish exercising at least three hours before you go to bed so the extra adrenaline won't be pumping through your bloodstream while you're trying to fall asleep.

WHEN IS THE BEST TIME TO DRINK WATER IF YOU'RE GOING TO EXERCISE? Before you exercise. Drink eight to sixteen ounces within an hour of exercise or your workout won't go as well, studies show. Then drink water during and after exercise to replenish the water you lose. Most people don't drink enough water to replace what they lose. **Sixty-four ounces a day?** A 2008 study that reviewed clinical studies about water consumption found no proof that drinking sixty-four ounces of water per day—a common recommendation—is necessary to keep the body adequately hydrated. In fact, the authors of the study couldn't even find a study that recommended drinking that much. There is some evidence, according to this study, that drinking lots of water helps the kidneys get rid of sodium and that water might control weight gain by helping to decrease appetite. But drinking too much water too fast can be dangerous, even fatal. **Tip:** Drinking decaffeinated coffee and tea and eating fruits and vegetables loaded with water also help hydrate your body.

WHEN IS THE BEST TIME TO APPLY SUNSCREEN? Fifteen to thirty minutes *before* you go into the sun. It takes time for your skin to absorb sunscreen, so apply it in advance. **Tip:** Assume all sunscreen will wash off during swimming no matter what the manufacturer claims. **Did you know?** Researchers have found that fair-skinned sunscreen users in the north may be more at risk for melanoma than those in the south. The researchers speculate that northern sunscreen users often don't feel the burning that would warn them to get out of the sun because the sun is less intense in the north. And while many sunscreens protect skin from UVB rays, they are less successful protecting skin from cancer-causing UVA rays, which are more of a threat to northerners who are in the sun longer. **FYI:** A 2008 study that tested nearly 1,000 sunscreen products found that more than 800 of them provided inadequate protection from the sun or included ingredients that might pose a health risk.

WHEN IS THE BEST TIME TO APPLY ICE TO SUNBURNS OR SCALDS? Never. Putting ice on a burn is an old wives' tale and does no more than provide some initial pain relief. In fact, icing a burn will slow the healing process, according to numerous studies. One study found that ice applied to the burn for ten minutes caused more damage to the skin than other ineffective burn remedies. It can also cause frostbite. **What to do?** Assuming it's a minor burn, immerse it in cold water, or run cold water over it, and then cover it with gauze but nothing else. Take a pain reliever if you need one.

WHEN IS THE BEST TIME TO CHEW GUM? Soon after eating. Chewing gum stimulates the flow of saliva, which neutralizes acids that cause tooth decay and contains minerals that strengthen teeth. The chewing motion also helps loosen food particles between teeth and removes plaque, which causes gingivitis. Dentists recommend chewing for fifteen minutes, but stick with sugarless gum. Sugar causes tooth decay and gum disease. **Another good time?** Right after colon surgery. In five studies with a total of 158 patients who had parts or all of their colons removed, some chewed sugarless gum three times a day for five to forty-five minutes, and some were not given gum. The gum chewers passed gas for the first time a half day earlier than nonchewers, experienced a bowel movement one day earlier, and left the hospital one day earlier. The researchers think chewing gum helps release hormones that help recovery, but other doctors caution that more study is needed. **FYI:** The first patent for chewing gum was issued in 1869 to William Semple, a dentist from Ohio.

WHEN IS THE BEST TIME TO STOP CHEWING NICOTINE GUM? Three months after you start using it. That's what the gum makers recommend. A small percentage of the people who use nicotine gum or lozenges become hooked on them, just as they were hooked on cigarettes.

WHEN IS THE BEST TIME FOR WOMEN TO QUIT SMOKING? During your period. A researcher who has studied success rates of women and their menstrual cycles found that women smokers were twice as likely to successfully quit smoking a few days after their periods began. **The worst time?** Two weeks before your period. If you try then, there is a seven out of ten chance you'll fail. Why? The theory is that Premenstrual Syndrome (PMS) symptoms, such as irritability and impulsiveness, may make it harder to quit.

WHEN IS THE BEST TIME IN YOUR LIFE TO HAVE YOUR HEARING TESTED? Before you're one month old. In fact, most hospitals won't discharge a newborn who hasn't been tested. The test used at most hospitals to check hearing examines the nerves that carry sound to the brain. **FYI:** About 12,000 babies are born each year in the United States with hearing problems.

WHEN IS THE BEST TIME TO HAVE YOUR EYES DILATED? Late afternoon. There technically isn't a time when your eyes will perform better in this test, but doctors say late afternoon is a more practical time. After dilation, it's best to go home and rest your eyes. Don't try to return to work or school and sit in front of a computer or try to read or write.

WHEN IS THE BEST TIME IN YOUR LIFE TO HAVE YOUR CHOLESTEROL TESTED? As early as age two and no later than ten, according to the American Academy of Pediatrics. The purpose for the early screening isn't to get children with high cholesterol on medication, though the academy believes that some children as young as eight can benefit from being medicated. But knowing about unhealthy cholesterol levels at an early age can alert doctors that a child needs to go on a special diet. What's more, children with high cholesterol levels often have parents with high cholesterol—a major contributor to deaths from coronary heart disease—so the screening of young children can alert doctors to potential health problems for the parents. **Another view:** Some doctors say fifteen months old is a good time to check cholesterol levels. Children often get vaccinations at that age, making it a convenient time for pediatricians to take a blood sample for cholesterol.

WHEN IS THE BEST TIME TO PUSH AWAY FROM THE THANKSGIVING DAY TABLE? After about 1,500 calories. At that point, the stomach says enough already and releases a hormone that causes nausea. **By the way:** The average American takes in about 4,500 calories—and 229 grams of fat—on Turkey Day. That compares to the 3,750 or so calories a day that Americans usually consume. **FYI:** During the rest of the year, Americans take in about 100 more calories a day than Italians, 200 more than Canadians, 300 more than Brits, 600 more than Mexicans, 800 more than the Chinese, and 1,300 more than Indians.

WHEN IS THE BEST TIME IN YOUR LIFE TO HAVE A FLAT STOMACH? In your forties. It has been well documented that fat around the waist leads to an increased risk for diabetes and heart disease. Now it appears that fortysomethings with a potbelly also are more likely to suffer from dementia later in life, according to a study of 6,583 men and women who were in their forties from 1964 to 1973. When participants were checked about thirty years later, 1,049 of them had dementia. The people with the largest waistlines were nearly three times more likely to suffer from dementia than those with the smallest waistlines. Those with forty-inch waistlines were twice as likely to have dementia than those with the flattest stomachs.

WHEN IS THE BEST TIME FOR A WOMAN TO PUT ON A LITTLE WEIGHT? During the transition to menopause. A study of 373 menopausal women over five years found that women who maintained their weight or lost a few pounds during this time also experienced enough bone loss to increase the risk of a fracture. Women who gained weight did not. The deciding factor here is estrogen, the main sex hormone in women that regulates the menstrual cycle and contributes to the development of female characteristics such as breasts, increased fat in the lower body, smooth skin, and less facial and body hair. After menopause, estrogen is mostly generated in fat tissue. Less fat means lower estrogen levels, and lower estrogen levels mean more rapid bone less. **What to do?** The solution is not to gain a lot of weight. Take vitamin D and calcium supplements daily, and work out with weights for at least thirty minutes two or three times a week. The weight you gain should be from larger muscles, not more fat.

WHEN IS THE BEST TIME TO WEIGH YOURSELF? Whatever time you pick. There is no best time of day or day of the week to weigh yourself because your weight fluctuates based on factors such as food consumption and water retention. That means you can weigh yourself before you go to sleep at night and then first thing in the morning and discover you've actually gained weight while you slept. Whenever you decide to weigh yourself, stick to that time. **Other tips:** 1) Scales can be inconsistent, so use the same scale every time. 2) Weigh yourself no more than twice a week to reduce the chances that normal fluctuations will discourage you.

WHICH IS THE BEST MONTH TO GET A FLU SHOT? October. Although flu season can begin that early, it usually begins in November. Because a flu shot usually takes about two weeks to start protecting you, getting one in October will provide protection throughout flu season, which usually lasts through March. The longer you wait, the better the chance you'll get the flu, so why wait? **Tips:** 1) Get a flu shot every year. The vaccine typically protects your body for only about six months. Also, flu strains change all the time, as do the vaccines that fight them. 2) Flu season can stretch into April, so if you haven't gotten a flu shot in October or November, it's not too late to get one in December or January. 3) To be safe, get a flu shot whenever you travel abroad, even if it's not flu season where you're going. **FYI:** The flu bug spreads fastest when the temperature is at 41 degrees F and humidity is at 35 percent or less, according to a study of flu-afflicted guinea pigs.

WHEN IS THE BEST TIME TO TAKE AN ASPIRIN TO CONTROL HIGH BLOOD PRESSURE? At bedtime. Doctors often advise taking aspirin to control high blood pressure, but blood pressure usually drops at night, so why then? Hormones and other chemicals that cause high blood pressure are most active at night, so you want aspirin in your body then to try to control them. A study presented in 2008 confirmed this, finding that high blood pressure sufferers benefit more from taking aspirin at night.

WHEN IS THE BEST TIME TO TAKE PAIN-RELIEF MEDICATION? When you first feel the pain. If you wait too long, it may not work well. **Tip:** Take pain medication before starting a strenuous activity, such as lifting weights, shoveling snow, or a physically demanding home-improvement project.

WHEN IS THE BEST TIME TO TAKE ASTHMA MEDICINE AND INHALERS? Six in the morning. Asthma attacks occur when the tubes that carry air to the lungs narrow, and those tubes are often at their narrowest between 6 a.m. and 8:00 a.m. Head that off with treatment. By the way, the tubes typically are at their widest between 4 p.m. and 6:00 p.m. **Did you know?** A new study, though inconclusive, shows that children who do not attend day care are more likely to suffer from asthma by age five than those who go to day care. The theory is that children in day care are more likely to be exposed to germs and infections that protect them from asthma.

WHEN IS THE BEST TIME OF THE DAY FOR AN ASTHMATIC TO SEE A DOCTOR? In the morning, the first appointment of the day if possible. Testing airway function in the afternoon, when tubes are at their widest, may not help doctors determine the severity of the asthma, but a morning appointment, when tubes are narrowest, may confirm it.

WHEN IS THE BEST TIME OF THE DAY TO TREAT MIGRAINE HEADACHES? In the morning. Finding the right drugs to treat migraines can be a nightmare, but if you've found something that works for you, take it as soon as you wake up. Migraine symptoms often peak between 6 a.m. and noon.

WHEN IS THE BEST TIME OF THE DAY TO TREAT HAY FEVER? In the morning, for the same reason that that's the best time to treat migraines. The worst symptoms come between 5 a.m. and 7 a.m. but often last into the late morning.

WHEN IS THE BEST TIME OF DAY TO EAT FRUIT? First thing in the morning. Fruit contains plenty of water, natural sugar, vitamins, and antioxidants, so you can make a pretty good argument for eating it any time throughout the day. But fruit is an excellent source of energy, and your body turns to your muscles for energy in the morning. Nutritionists also recommend eating fruit between meals because it is digested very quickly, doesn't stay in your stomach very long, and won't spoil your appetite.

WHEN IS THE BEST TIME OF DAY TO EAT FOOD RICH IN PROTEINS, SUCH AS TURKEY, EGGS, NUTS, AND FISH? The morning and at lunch. Plenty of evidence shows that protein supplies your body with energy so you can make it through the day, and it maintains your body tissues. You can live without carbohydrates but not without protein.

WHEN IS THE BEST TIME OF DAY TO EAT CARBOHYDRATES? At night. Carbohydrates—found in sugary or starchy foods such as bread, pasta, sweet corn and fruit—help support the nighttime chemistry of the body by providing your body with energy while you rest. Just don't eat a whole lot of them. If you do, you may gain weight. After 4 p.m., cut back on proteins and eat foods loaded with carbs. A small amount of sweets is okay, too; half a pie is not.

WHEN IS THE BEST TIME OF THE DAY TO EAT STARCHY VEGETABLES? Late afternoon and night. Tuberous vegetables, such as potatoes, sweet potatoes, and yams, are as starchy as you can get and should be eaten at night for the same reason other carbohydrates are best eaten at night. Most vegetables are not particularly starchy and can be eaten throughout the day. A number of fruits that we treat as vegetables, such as pumpkins, squash, cucumbers, tomatoes, and peppers, might seem starchy, but they're made up mostly of water and can be eaten at any time of the day.

WHEN IS THE BEST TIME OF THE DAY TO EAT FOODS RICH IN B VITAMINS, SUCH AS BANANAS, AVOCADOS, AND SUNFLOWER SEEDS? The evening. These foods help the body produce tryptophan, an amino acid that induces sleep.

WHEN IS THE BEST TIME OF THE DAY TO TAKE VITAMIN B_1? With dinner, assuming you eat most of your carbohydrates then. Vitamin B_1 is great at breaking down carbs, and it works best when taken with food.

WHEN IS THE BEST TIME OF THE DAY TO TAKE FOLIC ACID? Bedtime. This B vitamin, which is found naturally in leafy green vegetables, dried beans, peas, and certain fruits, works best when we sleep, repairing and regenerating the body. **Did you know?** Women of child-bearing age can reduce their risk of having a baby born with a serious birth defect of the brain and spine by as much as 70 percent if they take folic acid before and during the first three months of pregnancy.

WHEN IS THE BEST TIME TO TAKE A MULTIVITAMIN? Breakfast time. This vitamin absorbs into the body better with food. If you're going to take a multivitamin with a meal, breakfast makes the most sense because most people eat breakfast at home, where they're more likely to have vitamins around.

WHEN IS THE BEST TIME OF THE DAY TO TAKE MAGNESIUM AND CALCIUM SUPPLEMENTS? Right before bed. They have a calming effect and may help you get to sleep. The daily allowance for calcium is between 800 and 1,300 milligrams per day, depending on your age, or roughly three to four eight-ounce glasses of milk.

WHEN IS THE BEST TIME OF THE DAY TO TAKE ZINC SUPPLEMENTS? When your stomach is empty—either first thing in the morning, between meals, or before bed. Unlike multivitamins, zinc is absorbed best in the body when there is little or nothing in your stomach. **FYI:** These days, more and more people are taking zinc, a mineral that helps your body with immunity functions, because some research has shown that it helps some people battle the common cold. Although there have been more than a hundred major studies on the effectiveness of zinc during the past two decades, it's still unclear whether it does much to fight colds. If you think it works for you, take zinc as soon as possible after the first cold symptoms surface. Many people swear by zinc lozenges, but if you take a supplement, be on the safe side and take a small dose, say 25 milligrams. Too much zinc can interfere with immune system function and reduce the level of high-density lipoprotein (HDL, or "good" cholesterol). The safe upper limit of zinc intake for adults is 40 milligrams, and from 4 to 34 milligrams for children, depending on their age. **And finally:** Good sources of zinc include oysters, red meat, poultry, beans, nuts, whole grains, fortified breakfast cereals, and dairy products.

WHEN IS THE BEST TIME OF DAY TO TAKE MELATONIN? Five in the afternoon. Melatonin has been called the "Dracula hormone" because it is released during darkness—mostly between 11 p.m. and 7 a.m.—and helps people sleep. If you're trying to get to sleep earlier, take a melatonin supplement in the late afternoon and keep the lights dim in the early evening. Although melatonin will make some people groggy quickly, most people need to be in a place where the lights are dim in order for it to be effective. Bright light negates its effect. If you take melatonin and hang out in dim light, you should have no problem falling asleep fifteen minutes to a half hour earlier than usual. Some brands are stronger than others, so make sure you know what you're taking. **Did you know?** A study of 2,978 women over the age of seventy found that those who slept five hours or less per night were about 47 percent more likely to fall down more than those who slept seven or eight hours. But a study of about 93,000 postmenopausal women found that sleeping nine or more hours a night increased the risk of stroke by 70 percent. Why? The researchers said the extra sleep could throw the body's internal clock out of whack, leading to heartbeat abnormalities or problems with the arteries leading to the brain.

CHAPTER SIX

READING, WRITING, AND 'RITHMETIC

An experienced public school teacher once said that in an ideal world children would be taught subjects when they're most passionate about them. She knew most second graders love dinosaurs, so she taught lesson after lesson about dinosaurs and discovered that her students became more interested in science and geography. They also became better spellers because they wanted to learn how to spell tyrannosaurus, velociraptor, triceratops, and other dinosaur names. Children don't all learn at the same pace, but that doesn't mean timing is an insignificant part of how they process information. On the contrary.

WHEN IS THE BEST TIME FOR PRESCHOOLERS TO LEARN? The morning. Studies show many children who go to preschool in the morning are better adjusted to school than children who go in the afternoon. And a study of 154 preschool teachers in Greece reported half as many behavior problems in the morning than in the afternoon. Why? It could be because preschoolers, like everyone else, get tired in the early afternoon and find it more difficult to focus their attention. Teachers and school administrators at all levels acknowledge this reality, and many full-day preschools accommodate children by scheduling a nap time in the early afternoon.

WHEN IS THE BEST TIME OF THE DAY FOR OTHER STUDENTS TO LEARN? It's a three-way tie, according to one study, which came to the conclusion that 30 percent learn best in the mornings, 30 percent learn best in the afternoons, 30 percent learn best at night, and 10 percent have no preference. That means when the school day starts, only as many as 40 percent of children are at their intellectual peaks. Same goes for the afternoons. Other studies show similar breakdowns, making it difficult to pinpoint a precise answer. But one study of 103 high school dropouts in Washington state found that they preferred learning in the evening and said they found it difficult to learn in the morning.

WHEN IS THE BEST TIME TO SEND CHILDREN TO FULL-DAY SCHOOL? Age four. Or maybe seven. This is an extremely difficult question to answer, because our brains are each wired differently and develop differently. Some children are just not able to begin reading, writing, and computing when teachers and school administrators expect them to do those things, while others do it before they're asked to. That said, plenty of thick books have been written with the sole purpose of answering this question. The mountains of scholarship have led to compelling arguments for ages four and seven, so here they are (in the tiniest of nutshells):

Why four? Numerous studies show that children who start attending full-day preschool at age four are more likely to be able to read by the time they start kindergarten. And being able to read in kindergarten gives children an enormous amount of confidence, which very often translates into liking school, wanting to be there, and succeeding. This is especially true for academically at-risk students, some of whom wouldn't otherwise hold a book or a pencil until kindergarten. Other studies show that children who attend full-time preschool do better in math until the age of ten (at least) than their peers who didn't start school as early. As a result of these benefits, hundreds of millions of dollars are being spent to open public preschools in the United States and elsewhere, though most American children still start full-day school at five. **Did you know?** Children in Northern Ireland start school at four. Children in England, Malta, the Netherlands, Scotland, and Wales start at five, while those in Austria, Belgium, Cyprus, Czech Republic, Greece, Hungary, Iceland, Ireland, Italy, Liechtenstein, Luxembourg, Norway, Portugal, Romania, Slovakia, Slovenia, Spain, and Turkey start at six.

Why seven? A well-regarded study of children in thirty-two countries found that students who started school later did better. In fact, Finnish children, who start at seven, recently beat high school students from thirty-nine other countries in math, science, and reading. Other studies have found that children who start school later catch up—often by age eight or nine—with students who got an earlier start. And other studies show that sending children to school at four or five can breed a sense of failure and boredom that can be difficult, if not impossible, to shake. It's worth noting that many countries that start full-time school at seven start sending their children to part-time preschool when they're toddlers. **Other countries that start at seven:** Bulgaria, Estonia, Denmark, Latvia, Lithuania, Poland, and Sweden.

WHEN IS THE BEST TIME OF THE DAY FOR STUDENTS TO STUDY SOMETHING THAT THEY'LL REMEMBER FOR A LONG TIME? From 8 p.m. to midnight. The nervous system is particularly aroused at about 8 p.m., and long-term memory improves during this arousal period.

Researchers theorize that when the nervous system is aroused, the brain pays more attention to information it finds important and interesting.

WHEN IS THE BEST TIME OF THE DAY FOR STUDENTS TO STUDY SOMETHING THAT THEY NEED TO REMEMBER FOR A SHORT TIME? From 9 a.m. to 11 a.m. Short-term memory is about 15 percent more efficient in the late morning. At this time, the brain—for reasons unclear to researchers—cares less about what's important and interesting, so students are less likely to have a long-term memory of information studied for the first time at this time. In a study of British school children, two groups of students were read the same story, one at 9 a.m. and the other at 3 p.m. The students who heard the story at 9 a.m. did a better job of immediately recalling details of the story than did the students who heard the story at 3 p.m. But seven days later, the students who had heard the story at 3 p.m. recalled more details than did the students who had heard the story at 9 a.m. **FYI:** College students unknowingly take advantage of this rhythm by staying up late studying, then doing a quick review in the morning before the exam. But researchers say sleep plays a key role. A good night's sleep improves memory, while too little sleep hinders the brain's ability to encode new memories.

WHEN IS THE BEST TIME TO LEARN HANDWRITING? As soon as a child is able. Writing and thinking go hand in hand, studies show, and children who don't work on penmanship early enough often have more trouble writing letters as they age. Some children who don't practice penmanship enough also increase the likelihood that they'll have trouble with spelling and arithmetic, studies show. Some researchers attribute this to a poorly understood link between penmanship and other academic subjects, while others say the link is actually pretty simple: Students who are willing to put in the time to master penmanship are more likely to do the same when it comes to studying spelling words, doing math drills, and learning science, geography, and other subjects. Many education traditionalists fear that proper penmanship is becoming a lost art as children become more and more proficient using computer keyboards. **Did you know?** National Handwriting Day is January 23. Why January 23? That's the birthday of the guy with arguably the world's most famous signature: John Hancock. A group called the Writing Instrument Manufacturers Association suggests that on January 23, everyone make a point of using a pen or a pencil to write a note, poem, letter, or journal entry.

WHEN IS THE BEST TIME TO LEARN A FOREIGN LANGUAGE? As a child. In fact, lots of people who learn to speak foreign languages before puberty speak them without an accent, while those who learn to speak a foreign language after puberty, such as diplomat Henry Kissinger and actor and politician Arnold Schwarzenegger, never lose their accents. That's because the so-called language centers in your brain lose flexibility around puberty and won't allow you to speak a second language without an accent. But research shows if you learn three languages before puberty, your language centers will remain flexible and you'll be able to learn more languages later in life, often without an accent. **FYI:** No one disputes that children's brains can soak up lots of information, including foreign vocabularies, but some children who are exposed to more than one language take a very long time to truly master one of them, and some never do.

WHEN IS THE BEST TIME FOR AN ADULT TO LEARN A FOREIGN LANGUAGE? In the weeks before you have the chance to use it. If you learn it and then don't use it for a while, it will most likely fade from your mind, leaving you with only a handful of words and phrases. **Tips for best results:** 1) Go where the language is spoken, if possible, so you can immerse yourself in the language. If you want to learn Italian, for example, but you don't have the time and money to go to Italy, then drive to the Little Italy in the city nearest to where you live or visit nearby Italian-American clubs where the language is spoken. 2) Record a thirty-minute news show in the language you want to learn and watch it over and over again, each time writing down every word you hear, then translating it into your native tongue. 3) Buy a language-learning kit with tapes or CDs.

WHEN IS THE BEST TIME TO LEARN MATH? Right after class. You need to pay attention during class, of course, but researchers have found that students who review what they just heard for ten to fifteen minutes after class are more likely to remember it and successfully apply it. In fact, reviewing right after class allows math students to recall 83 percent of class discussion nine weeks later, studies show. Retention plummets to 14 percent when students wait even one day to do a review. **FYI:** Researchers have found that it takes about seventeen seconds of close attention to remember something, so don't rush while you're doing your review.

WHEN IS THE BEST TIME OF DAY TO TAKE A TEST? Ten in the morning. This is one of those times of day when most people feel alert and up to just about any challenge. And even if you skip breakfast, the stress hormone cortisol rises while you sleep, increasing your blood sugar and giving you some energy. **Tip:** If you're scheduled to take a test in the late morning, review the material on the test right before. Short-term memory is more efficient then.

WHEN IS THE BEST TIME OF THE DAY TO DO HOMEWORK? About thirty minutes after students get home from school. Most children need a break after they get home. Give them a snack, let them unwind, and ask them about their day. Some children also like to change their clothes to complete the transition from school to home. Doing these things makes many children feel rested and ready to do their homework. With younger students, you want to get homework out of the way before dinnertime. Older students may not be able to get everything done between the end of their school day and dinner, but getting some of it done not long after they get home will make it more likely that your teen will not stay up all night doing homework. **Tip:** You know your children better than anyone, so if this time doesn't work for them, try different times until you find the right one.

WHEN IS THE BEST TIME TO START TEACHING YOUR CHILD ABOUT THE BIRDS AND THE BEES? Around age five or six. Don't bother with the once-obligatory "big sit-down sex talk" when your child turns thirteen or fourteen. That's way too late. Most children start asking sex-related questions when they're five or six, and you should be ready with age-appropriate answers. Sex education needs to be an ongoing conversation in which parents repeatedly share their values about relationships and sex. Experts say these conversations won't make your child more likely to have sex. In fact, if your message to your kids involves waiting, they'll be more likely to wait. **Tips:** 1) Listen to your child and encourage questions. 2) Realize you don't have all the answers, and admit that—but then go find the answers. 3) Make sure your child knows you love him or her no matter what.

WHEN IS THE BEST TIME OF DAY FOR TEENAGERS TO ATTEND SCHOOL? From 9:30 a.m. to 4:30 p.m. When researchers released findings that showed that teens' sleep patterns often cause them to want to go to bed later and wake up later, a relatively small number of school districts, most notably Minneapolis, moved back start times by an hour or so. In many of those school districts, administrators saw more well-rested and relaxed students, less absenteeism and tardiness, and better grades. In Lexington, Kentucky, where start times were delayed one hour for middle and high school students, researchers reported that car accidents for teen drivers there decreased while they increased elsewhere in Kentucky. But most school districts have balked at the change, citing logistical problems involving transportation and the need for students to work after-school jobs and participate in extracurricular activities. **Did you know?** Researchers have found that one out of fourteen adolescents suffers from something called delayed sleep-phase syndrome—a form of insomnia more severe than the normal sleep patterns of their peers—that keeps them from falling asleep as early as they should.

WHEN IS THE BEST TIME OF DAY FOR STUDENTS TO EAT LUNCH AT SCHOOL? Not 9:05 a.m. That's when one high school in Virginia Beach began serving lunch a few years back because administrators there said scheduling dilemmas left them with no choice. Seven other high schools in Virginia Beach—and many others in southeast Virginia—began serving lunch before 10 a.m., prompting the Virginia Department of Education to remind school districts to comply with federal guidelines that call for serving lunch between 10 a.m. and 2 p.m. So when is the best time? There has been very little research on this, but many students, teachers, and administrators say before 11 a.m. is too early and after 1 p.m. is too late. **Did you know?** In high schools across the country where administrators are concerned that many students skip lunch or don't have enough time in their schedules for a lunch period, they are creating mandatory lunch periods. A Catholic school south of San Francisco requires students to eat lunch and schedules a thirty-minute snack break at 10:45 a.m. In nearby Palo Alto, an all-girls school with a mandatory lunch period sets out milk and fresh fruit all day and serves granola bars and other healthy snacks in the afternoon.

WHEN IS THE BEST TIME OF DAY TO TRY OUT FOR A SPORTS TEAM? Between 5 p.m. and 7 p.m. Several things are happening in your body to make this the best time: This is when your lungs use oxygen more efficiently, you're more coordinated, your muscles have the most potential to perform at their peak, and you are at your peak for flexibility. That's the good news. The bad news is if you're trying out during this time, chances are so is everyone else, so you won't have an advantage.

WHEN IS THE BEST TIME FOR ATHLETES TO LEARN A TRICKY NEW PLAY? Three in the afternoon. That's according to scientists who schedule the work of astronauts at NASA's Biomedical Research Division. At that time, the scientists say, athletes, both young and old, are more likely to learn a new play well because they are alert and entering a phase in the day when they feel physically prepared to execute it. However, if they are taught the play at 9 a.m., the team's ability to recall the play will be as if they had slept for only three hours the night before and are not as alert as they should be. It's also true that long-term memory is sharper at 3 p.m. than at most other times of the day.

WHEN IS THE BEST TIME OF DAY TO HOLD A PEP RALLY? Three in the afternoon, or right before the school day ends. A dip in body temperature in the early afternoon can cause drowsiness, but a rise in body temperature makes you more alert and energetic later in the afternoon. You also have a fair amount of energy in the late morning, but the excitement from a pep rally boosts adrenaline and makes it hard to return to the classroom, so the very end of the school day is best. **Did you know?** More and more schools are holding pep rallies to help motivate students who are about to take standardized tests. Administrators say it helps children understand the importance of doing well on the tests, and it shines a spotlight on academics.

WHEN IS THE BEST TIME TO SURPRISE STUDENTS DURING A LESSON OR LECTURE? Every ten minutes. That's about how long students will give their attention to their teachers and professors after a class begins. Why ten minutes? Brain researchers don't know for sure, but a college professor who split his fifty-minute lectures into five ten-minute lectures, each with their own "hooks," has won accolades for this method, which helps him retain the attention of his students.

WHEN IS THE BEST TIME FOR PROSPECTIVE STUDENTS TO VISIT COLLEGES? While college is in session. Some like to go in the summers when the pace is more leisurely and orientation tour groups often are small. But visiting colleges in the summer will give you only part of the picture. Go while most students are there so you'll get a better feel for how the college really operates. The vast majority of colleges offer classes in the summer—in fact, more and more students are taking classes then—but it's a scaled-back time, when labs, studios, and theaters go unused, sporting events aren't happening, and cafeterias offer the bare minimum. **Tip:** Don't wait until you're in the eleventh or twelfth grade to take a campus tour. More and more tenth graders are visiting colleges in order to give themselves more time to figure out where to apply.

WHEN IS THE BEST TIME TO APPLY FOR COLLEGE? The fall. Application deadlines vary from college to college, but twelfth graders who apply in the fall under "early decision" programs often increase their chances of getting into the universities of their choice. College admissions officials tend to take these applications more seriously because they often require students to decide whether or not to commit to the college soon after they get accepted, and colleges want to reward students for making that commitment early. These students find out where they'll attend college by mid-December, so they don't have that huge question hanging over their heads during the winter holidays, not to mention the last semester of high school. But there's a catch: If accepted, students almost always must attend, though some universities will let students back out of their commitment if they believe they can't afford it or they determine the students were forced by their parents to apply. **Note:** Harvard, Princeton, and the University of Virginia, to name three, eliminated early decision in an attempt to make the admissions process fairer to students who aren't prepared to begin applying in the fall.

WHEN IS THE BEST MONTH TO SUBMIT PAPERWORK FOR FEDERAL STUDENT AID? January. The deadline to submit the federal student aid application, the holy grail of student aid applications, is June 30, but there won't be much money left by then. In fact, there won't be much money left by April. The Free Application for Federal Student Aid, widely known as FAFSA, can't be submitted until January 1, but don't wait past the middle of February, when many colleges expect to see your application. Colleges make most admissions offers in mid- to late March—most have a deadline of April 1—and they want to help prospective students, particularly the most sought-after ones, make up their minds by letting them know then how much financial aid they'll receive.

WHEN IS THE BEST TIME TO MEET WITH A PROFESSOR? As soon as you realize you're in trouble in the class. Don't wait until you've dug yourself too deep a hole. Find out when the professor offers office hours, or make an appointment if the office hours are inconvenient for you. Professors want to know that you care, and making an effort to talk with them is a good way to do that. **More tips from profs:** 1) Be polite and address your professor with respect. You have nothing to gain by being rude, even if he's late for your appointment. 2) Don't ask for an extra credit assignment unless you know your professor is known to offer them. 3) Don't tell your professor that you *need* a certain grade to keep a scholarship or stay on a sports team. That's not the professor's problem.

WHEN IS THE BEST TIME OF YEAR TO SELL USED BOOKS TO A COLLEGE BOOK STORE? Mid-August through the first week of September and late November through mid-January. At colleges on semester schedules, professors usually let the bookstores know by early August which books they plan to use in the fall semester and by mid-November which books they plan to use for the spring semester. In order to get more of these books, many college bookstores often will pay 50 percent the cost of a book as long as the used book they're buying is in good condition. Many colleges have "Buyback Week," which usually coincides with finals week, or the last week of the semester. If your college does, make sure you go as soon as possible. The bookstores have quotas to buy, and when they reach those quotas, they may be uninterested in your books, or they may offer you pennies on the dollar for them. **Money-saving tips:** 1) More and more college students are renting their textbooks, saving as much as 80 percent of the cost of a new textbook. Companies such as Chegg.com, Campusbookrentals.com, and Bookrenter.com make it easy to rent, but make sure you comparison shop and know how much shipping and handling will cost. 2) Consider buying e-books, which you can download to your computer or to an e-reader. They sometimes cost less than traditional books and come with audio and video extras.

WHEN IS THE BEST TIME TO MAKE PAYMENTS ON A FEDERALLY SUBSIDIZED STUDENT LOAN? During the grace period. If you can pay then, go ahead and do it. You'll pay no interest and every dollar goes toward the principal. That's the equivalent of a short-term, no-interest loan from Mom and Dad. If you owe $10,000 on a ten-year loan with a 5 percent interest rate and pay nothing during the grace period, the loan will cost you $12,905 if you repay it over ten years. However, if you pay $1,000 during the grace period, the loan will cost you $12,614 over ten years—a savings of $291. If your loan is unsubsidized, the interest continues to compound during your grace period. **Another view:** Start repaying the loan only when you must. The interest on many student loans is tax deductible. Check with a tax consultant. **Money-saving tip:** Stafford loan recipients who consolidate their loans may be able to reduce the interest rate by a half percentage point or more.

CHAPTER SEVEN

SERIOUS STUFF

Spending your money, taking care of your health, running your business, or educating your kids is far from fluff. But this chapter delves into how timing plays a role in a cornucopia of serious issues that can affect the rest of your life. This chapter suggests, among other things, the best time to be married, have kids, buy a house, invest in the stock market, pay taxes, file a lawsuit, have surgery, and collect Social Security benefits.

WHICH IS THE BEST MONTH TO MARRY? June. Okay, this very well may be the fuzziest answer in this book. But for starters, the Roman goddess Juno—June's namesake—was given domain over marriage and birth, and at one time, that meant something to families who wanted their daughters to have happy marriages and lots of kids. For more practical reasons, the weather is warm and pleasant in June in most of the Northern Hemisphere, and school may be out, allowing families with children a better chance to travel to out-of-town weddings.

WHEN IS THE BEST TIME IN YOUR LIFE TO BE IN A MARRIAGE? Middle age. A study of the physical effects of loneliness found that sustained loneliness in people ages fifty to sixty-eight led to increased blood pressure and other health problems. The United States is becoming a lonelier place—one in four Americans can't name a trusted friend—so understanding the health effects of loneliness will become more important as baby boomers age. But not just any old spouse will do, according to another study, which found that while happily married people tend to have lower blood pressure than nonmarried folks, single people may be healthier than those in unhappy marriages. Yet another study found that the health of those who never married improved from 1972 to 2004, while the health gap between married and never-married men narrowed. The health gap did not narrow for women.

WHEN IS THE BEST TIME FOR CAREER-ORIENTED WOMEN TO START HAVING KIDS? Early adulthood. Sociologists who study this have come up with a logical decision model, and one of the logical decisions calls for having children early in your career. Why? For one thing, maternity leave has less impact on the career of someone just starting her career. And second, the children will be older and more independent by the time their mother's career has blossomed and requires her to work more hours.

WHEN IS THE BEST TIME TO MAKE LOVE WITH THE INTENT OF GETTING PREGNANT? About three hours before ovulation. The sperm need to be released and waiting for the eggs, which only live for twelve hours or so. Fortunately, sperm can live for two to five days, so having sex as many as five days before ovulation can lead to pregnancy. That's still a relatively short window of opportunity, so to give yourselves a better chance, you'll need as many sperm as possible to be ready to pounce on an egg. That means you males should refrain from ejaculating for two days before ovulation is most likely to occur. **Other tips:** Don't drink, smoke, or take drugs when you're trying to get pregnant. And you females actually have more power than you may realize: You can actually move the sperm along by having an orgasm during or right after the male's orgasm. **How about having sex a day after ovulation?** It may be great fun, but if you do it then, don't count on fertilizing an egg.

WHICH IS THE BEST MONTH TO GET PREGNANT? August. This one, no doubt, is debatable, but here are two practical arguments for August: 1) Getting pregnant then means you'll probably have a May baby, and you won't be several months pregnant during the long, hot summer months. 2) The worst morning sickness for pregnant women usually occurs during the first three months, so conceiving in August usually means the worst bouts of nausea will be a thing of the past by the winter holidays, when people tend to socialize more. So even if you can't have wine with Thanksgiving dinner or a cocktail at a Christmas party, at least you won't have to worry about being nauseous then.

WHICH IS THE BEST DAY OF THE WEEK TO GIVE BIRTH? Any day as long as it's not on the weekend. Saturdays and Sundays appear to have the highest mortality rates. Why? Hospitals are better staffed on weekdays. That helps explain why mothers who have the luxury of picking the day their babies are born—because their deliveries are induced by drugs or because they are delivering by a scheduled Caesarian section—often choose weekdays or are advised to do so. Pregnant women who arrive at hospitals on weekends may not enjoy all the benefits of a fully staffed hospital, and while that's usually not a problem, if there's a complication, it could become one.

WHEN IS THE BEST TIME TO STOP RENTING AND BUY A HOUSE? When it costs less to buy than to rent. And how do you figure that out? Find two similar houses—one for sale and one for rent—and divide the asking price by the annual rent. The answer is the rent ratio. During the 1970s, 1980s, and 1990s, the nationwide rent ratio stayed between 10 and 14, then rose to nearly 19 in 2006, when the housing market topped out. (The rent ratio neared 35 in San Francisco and San Jose in 2006, among the highest in the nation back then.) A rent ratio of 20 or more usually means that it costs considerably more to own than to rent, once you factor in the mortgage, taxes, insurance, repairs, and other expenses. Ideally, you'll buy when the rent ratio is a lot closer to 10 than to 20.

WHICH IS THE BEST DAY OF THE YEAR TO MAKE AN OFFER ON A HOUSE? Christmas Day. Huh? Not all real estate agents agree, but those who do offer three reasons: 1) Sellers are in good and generous moods on Christmas, as are most people, and are more likely to come down on the price then. 2) Home prices are at a twelve-month low in December, and some sellers become more desperate as the month wears on without an offer. 3) Sellers are serious about selling this time of year—even on Christmas Day. The key is to find a real estate agent willing not only to work on Christmas but also to worm his or her way into the seller's house. An agent willing to do that for you is a go-getter who will help you close a deal that benefits you.

WHICH IS THE BEST DAY OF THE MONTH TO MAKE AN OFFER ON A HOUSE? The first Tuesday. Why early in the month? Because the homeowner just wrote a mortgage check for a house he no longer wants, and he doesn't want to write another one. Why Tuesday? Because he knows by Tuesday that he may not receive more offers from house hunters who saw the house the weekend before. (Many real estate agents swear by this, even though Christmas Day will never fall on the first Tuesday of December.)

WHICH IS THE BEST MONTH TO MAKE AN OFFER ON A HOUSE? January. Let's say your agent isn't aggressive enough to make an offer on your behalf on Christmas Day. Wait until January. There are fewer buyers willing to trudge through nasty weather looking at houses, so there's less competition and few, if any, bidding wars. And in January sellers tend to be more motivated to sell and more willing to accept a lower offer than they will be in the spring, when there are more serious buyers. Why? Two reasons: 1) They may have just received their credit card bills from Christmas and may be feeling financially insecure. 2) These sellers have decided not to wait for the spring to put their houses on the market, and that means they're willing to risk listing their houses during a time of the year when their properties won't show as well.

WHICH IS THE BEST DAY OF THE WEEK TO LIST YOUR HOUSE FOR SALE? Thursday. Why? Because your house will be available right away for weekend showings. By Saturday—the most important day of the real estate week—your house will have shown only two days. The fewer days on market, the better chance the home will attract a full-price offer. Even if your house doesn't sell until the following Saturday, it will still show only nine days on market, benefiting from the psychological advantage of a single-digit number.

WHEN IS THE BEST TIME OF THE YEAR TO SELL A HOUSE? Spring. It's true that there are more houses on the market then, but there also are more buyers, many of whom have been fantasizing about their dream homes all fall and winter. With tax refund checks in the bank, spring buyers more often pay full price. In fact, sales peak in the spring, leading to lots of summer closings. That helps explain why about 60 percent of those who move do so in the summer. **Money-saving tip:** Don't price your house with a zero at the end. A recent study shows that people perceive a precise price, such as $282,284, as lower than rounded ones, such as $280,000, even when the rounded prices are actually lower. Real-life sales showed that one or two zeros at the end of a price lowered the final sales price by 0.72 percent and 0.73 percent, respectively. That doesn't seem like much, but it can add up to thousands of dollars. For a company like Wal-Mart, which prices its goods this way, it adds up to many millions of dollars a year.

WHICH IS THE BEST MONTH TO START LISTING A LUXURY HOME FOR SALE? January. This is more true if you live in or near a big city where investment bankers and hedge fund managers receive huge end-of-the-year bonuses and start looking to make major purchases in early January. That also explains why sales of Bentleys, Ferraris, and other luxury vehicles are also up in January.

WHEN IS THE BEST TIME TO BUY FLOOD INSURANCE? Thirty days before you need it. That's because coverage usually doesn't begin until thirty days after you buy flood insurance. Find out if you need flood insurance at www.FloodSmart.gov, the Web site of the National Flood Insurance Program.

WHEN IS THE BEST TIME TO BUY LIFE INSURANCE? As soon as you become a parent. Or as soon as you get married, if your spouse doesn't have a job. If someone is depending on you to put food on the table and clothes in the closet, it's time to buy life insurance. The sooner you buy it, assuming you're in good health, the cheaper it is. The older and fatter and sicker you are, the more it costs. Don't wait until you're too sick or too old and become uninsurable. At that point, you won't be able to buy coverage, and your survivors will pay a steep price.

WHEN IS THE BEST TIME TO BUY STOCKS? As soon as you hear official word that a recession has arrived. Recessions tend to be recognized six to nine months after they begin. That means by the time a recession has been announced, most of the damage to the stock market has been done, so there are plenty of buying opportunities then. You can buy low, then wait for the economy to improve and sell high later.

WHEN IS THE BEST TIME OF DAY FOR A BEGINNER TO TRADE STOCKS? Between 11:00 a.m. and 2:00 p.m. The time when an investor makes a trade can affect the outcome of the trade. Don't trade first thing in the morning or late in the afternoon, when market volumes soar and prices can become volatile. Sure, you can make big money doing that, but if you really don't know what you're doing, you can also lose big money. The middle of the day tends to be the most calm and stable period for buying and selling stocks, since that's when people are waiting for news that may influence the market. And stable prices may lead to more predictable returns for investors.

WHEN IS THE BEST TIME TO START DIVERTING SOME OF YOUR PAYCHECK INTO A 401(K) ACCOUNT? The sooner, the better. Your 401(k) is what financial advisers and others call free money because you don't pay taxes on what you save while you're saving and because most employers match some of what you contribute. Here's an example that causes people to call their HR departments right away: A twenty-five-year-old who makes $40,000 a year invests $5,000 a year mostly in stocks that do only as well as the market average. Assuming that worker continues to save at that rate, he or she will retire forty years later with nearly $2 million.

WHEN IS THE BEST TIME TO CASH OUT YOUR 401(K)? Not until you're forced to do it. Let's say you leave a job with $50,000 in a 401(k) and you cash it out. You'll lose $20,000: $12,500 in federal taxes, assuming you're in the 25 percent tax bracket; $5,000 in an early-withdrawal penalty; and $2,500 in state taxes if the rate is 5 percent. That leaves you with $30,000. If you roll over that $50,000 into an IRA or into your new company's retirement plan and you earn a conservative 7 percent a year, you'll have $193,484 in twenty years.

WHEN IS THE BEST TIME TO COMPUTERIZE YOUR TAX PREPARATION? The next time you do it. The IRS estimates that a preparer in an average household will spend fourteen to sixteen hours completing Form 1040 the old-fashioned way, not including Schedule A or D. Those who use tax preparation software can do it in about four hours.

WHEN IS THE BEST TIME TO FILE YOUR TAX FORMS IF YOU'RE OWED A REFUND? Before the middle of March, if possible. That's when accounting and IRS offices start getting incredibly busy. Accountants say it takes longer and longer to get through to anyone at the IRS starting at the beginning of February. **Tips:** File electronically if you can, and instruct the IRS to deposit your return directly in your bank account. You'll get your money a bit faster. **Did you know?** Nearly three out of every four returns from taxpayers who are owed money arrive at the IRS before April 1.

WHEN IS THE BEST TIME TO FILE YOUR TAX FORMS IF YOU OWE MONEY? April 14 or 15. Why not hang onto your money as long as possible, right? **Tip:** Play it safe and send it certified mail/return receipt so, if need be, you can prove you beat the deadline. **Did you know?** The IRS receives about six out of every ten "balance-due returns" after April 15.

WHEN IS THE BEST TIME OF DAY TO BREAK BAD NEWS TO SOMEONE? In the evening. You may not have a choice of when you drop a bomb on someone, but if you do, try the evening, when blood pressure and heart rate drop. **The worst time?** In the morning. Heart attacks are much more likely to occur between 6 a.m. and noon, when blood pressure and heart rate peak. This unfortunate combination puts stress on arterial walls, which, if blocked, can cause a heart attack. **Did you know?** A recent study of 117 college students who were asked to review other students' résumés found that the reviewers were more likely to offer negative feedback if they could use e-mail rather than a telephone. Why? The reviewers knew they wouldn't have to see and hear the potential pain caused by the negative feedback. However, the authors of the study recommend against using e-mail in highly personal situations, such as breaking up with your boyfriend or firing an employee.

WHICH IS THE BEST DAY OF THE WEEK TO FILE A LAWSUIT OR FILE FOR DIVORCE? Friday. Many lawyers say they like to serve papers—as well as engage in lengthy and potentially difficult conversations—at the end of the workweek because others tend to be in a better mood then. And they find they can often do better for their clients if their dealings with opposing lawyers are civil. **The worst month?** November or December. Lawyers don't want to file lawsuits or start difficult divorce proceedings right before or during the end-of-the-year holiday season. And many judges tend to take a lot of time off in December, forcing lawyers and their clients to wait until the new year for court dates, anyway.

WHEN IS THE BEST TIME OF THE DAY TO PERFORM DANGEROUS TASKS? Between 8 a.m. and noon and between 4 a.m. and 8 p.m. This has a lot to do with sleep patterns: You tend to be the most alert and have the most energy during these times of the day. **The worst time?** Early morning, particularly 4 a.m., is especially risky. Body temperature (which affects alertness) and concentration are at their lowest points at around 4 a.m. and studies show that time is associated with a nearly 100 percent increase in the incidence of work-related accidents. **The next worst time?** Early afternoon. At this time your chance of making mistakes rises by 50 percent as your body clock causes you to become less alert. **Did you know?** The Three Mile Island nuclear power plant accident—the most significant accident in the history of the American commercial nuclear power industry—began at exactly 4 a.m. on March 28, 1979.

WHEN IS THE BEST TIME OF THE DAY TO SPEED? At 8 a.m., 4 p.m., and midnight. Or whenever police and sheriff's department shift changes occur where you live. No one is advocating breaking the law, but sometimes our minds wander when we're behind the wheel, leading to our driving over the speed limit. The best time to do that is when police officers, including those on speed-trap duty, are either just getting off duty or just starting work, when they often haven't yet begun patrolling their areas.

WHEN IS THE BEST TIME OF THE DAY TO STAY OFF THE ROADS IN ORDER TO AVOID TRAFFIC AC-CIDENTS? From 8 a.m. to 9 a.m. and 5 p.m. to 6 p.m. Most accidents occur then—during morning and afternoon rush-hour traffic—so if you can avoid accidents then, you have a good shot of avoiding them altogether. Traffic density aside, it's twenty times more likely that an accident will occur at 6 a.m. than at 10 a.m. Attribute that to sleepy drivers. Studies show that fatigue leads to accidents involving younger drivers more often in the wee hours of the morning, whereas older drivers, who are less likely to be behind the wheel late at night and early in the morning, are more likely to get in fatigue-related accidents during afternoon rush-hour traffic. **Did you know?** If you feel tired all the time, it could be that your body clock isn't aligned with the demands of your life. Scientists at the University of California at Irvine have found that a single amino acid regulates your body clock, a discovery that could lead to the development of a drug that controls the brain's sleep cycle.

WHEN IS THE BEST TIME TO DRIVE AND TALK ON YOUR CELL PHONE? Never. One study found that you are four times more likely to get into an accident if you're driving while talking on a cell phone. Others found that drivers who use cell phones brake a half second slower during emergencies, miss more than half the visual cues on and along the road, and are more likely to tailgate other vehicles. That's a triple whammy that impedes drivers in the same way that driving drunk does. The study that found that cell phone users are four times more likely to get into accidents noted that 39 percent of those drivers, none of whom were injured, used their cell phones to call for help after their accidents. The other 61 percent made no calls or called friends or relatives. **FYI:** One study found that those who reach for something—not necessarily cell phones—while driving are nine times more likely to get in a crash or a near-crash.

WHEN IS THE BEST TIME OF THE DAY TO CALL THE POLICE AND EXPECT THEM TO SHOW UP QUICKLY?

Between 3 a.m. and 4 a.m. This time, otherwise known as "the dead hour," is when, according to one cop, "even most of the criminals are asleep." Dispatchers for 911 receive far fewer calls during this one-hour period, so it's more likely that your call, however minor, will receive prompt response from the police. This is not to say that crimes don't happen during this hour. They do, and sometimes they're quite serious. Many police departments make sure they have at least three-quarters of the number of officers working during the wee hours as they do during other, busier times of the day.

WHEN IS THE BEST TIME IN YOUR LIFE TO START MODERATELY DRINKING ALCOHOL? Middle age.

A study of 7,697 healthy people between the ages of forty-five and sixty-four—442 of whom were nondrinkers at the start of the study—found that the new drinkers were 38 percent less likely to suffer a heart-related event than those who drank no alcohol. On average, the new drinkers, none of whom abused alcohol, had lower cholesterol and lower blood pressure and experienced no increase in mortality. So if you're middle-aged and you don't drink alcohol, should you start now? Maybe, if you drink moderately, but don't start if your family history includes alcoholism.

WHEN IS THE BEST TIME OF THE DAY TO DRINK ALCOHOL RESPONSIBLY? The afternoon and evening. Plenty of studies show your body is better able to metabolize alcohol between 2 p.m. and 10 p.m., especially while you're eating dinner. **Did you know?** Canadian researchers who studied healthy adults found that one alcoholic beverage relaxed blood vessels and improved blood flow, while two made the heart work harder. Another study shows that just one drink at night can disrupt normal brain patterns while you sleep, causing bad dreams.

WHEN IS THE BEST TIME OF DAY TO SCHEDULE SURGERY? The morning. Studies show you're four times less likely to have surgery-related problems in the morning than between 3 p.m. and 4 p.m. Why? No one can say for sure, but early in the day, operating rooms are well stocked and prepped, doctors and nurses are generally well rested, and nothing yet has happened to delay or stress out surgeons and anesthesiologists. "It's the one time of the day when we're all on the same page," one operating room nurse said.

WHICH IS THE BEST DAY OF THE WEEK TO SEEK TREATMENT IN A HOSPITAL? Not the weekend. Recent studies have found that patients who go to the hospital during the week are better off than those who receive treatment during the weekend. A study of 231,164 heart attack patients at New Jersey hospitals found that those admitted during the weekend had a 12.9 percent mortality rate, compared with 12 percent for those admitted during the week. A study of 188,212 patients who had nonemergency surgeries on a Friday and who spent the weekend in the hospital were 17 percent more likely to die within thirty days than those who had their operations on a Monday, Tuesday, Wednesday, or Thursday. Researchers offer these theories: Weekend patients often put off getting treatment and tend to be sicker when they arrive at the hospital, and they may receive less aggressive treatment from less experienced doctors and nurses who are often assigned to weekend shifts.

WHEN IS THE BEST TIME OF THE MONTH TO GET A MAMMOGRAM? Not the week prior to your menstrual period. This is the time when most women's breasts are more tender or swollen, making the exam even more uncomfortable than it already is. Any other time of the month is better. **Tip:** Ask your doctor if you can get a digital mammogram instead of a traditional film mammogram. One study found that digital mammograms found early-stage and treatable malignancies not identified by film. **Did you know?** Breast cancer is more likely to develop in women fifty or older, and if you have other risk factors—Did your mother or sister develop breast cancer? Do you have mutations of certain genes, such as BRCA1, BRCA2, and p53?—start getting mammograms in your forties. Breast cancer can be very aggressive in younger women.

WHEN IS THE BEST TIME OF THE YEAR TO SCHEDULE A MAMMOGRAM? Exactly one year after the most recent one. If you postpone it by even two or three months, an aggressive cancer can thrive and do serious damage. So schedule the next one before you leave your doctor's office. Thanks largely to mammograms, the death rate from breast cancer has dropped 25 percent since 1990, but doctors are troubled that only 67 percent of women over forty received mammograms in 2005, down from 70 percent in 2000. Why? No one knows for sure, but researchers suspect it could have something to do with rising health insurance copayments, longer waits for appointments these days, and a feeling by some women that mammograms don't make much of a difference. And it doesn't help that mammograms can be uncomfortable. **FYI:** A recent study of more than 4,000 women sixty-five and older found that wealthier women—with a net worth of $100,000 or more—were more likely to get mammograms.

WHEN IS THE BEST TIME TO TELL YOUR DOCTOR IF YOU FEEL A LUMP? That day. While it's true that 60 percent of lumps in breasts are benign, you can't take that chance. Call your doctor, who will either see you immediately or refer you to a breast radiologist or a surgeon at a hospital or breast center. Also on that first day, call your insurer, who may require that you see your doctor before you go to a specialist. If you don't get a referral right away, you might be denied coverage for treatment later. Either way, you'll want to get a second opinion from an oncologist or radiologist at a hospital or cancer center. **Did you know?** Several studies show the discovery of breast cancer, a disease that will attack one out of nine women in America, is highest in the spring, the season when the cancer grows the fastest.

WHEN IS THE BEST TIME IN A WOMAN'S CYCLE TO HAVE A PAP SMEAR? Ten to twenty days after the start of your last period. A Pap smear, also known as a Pap test, checks for changes in the cells of your cervix and can tell if you have an infection, unhealthy cells, or cervical cancer. If you have a Pap smear during your menstrual period, menstrual fluid and blood may make it difficult for your doctor to interpret results. Putting anything inside the vagina—a penis, spermicides, or tampons—one to two days before the test can also affect the results. But even if you can't have the test done at the best time, doctors urge women not to cancel or reschedule—it's one of the most accurate cancer-detection tests. **FYI:** Women between twenty-one and thirty should have annual Pap smears—earlier than twenty-one if they're sexually active—and once every two or three years after thirty if your previous test results have been normal. **And finally:** A Greek doctor, George Nicolas Papanicolaou, invented the Pap smear.

WHEN IS THE BEST TIME TO HAVE YOUR BLOOD PRESSURE CHECKED? In the afternoon and when you're relaxed. Your blood pressure is at its highest in the morning, so wait until it calms down. If you must check it in the morning, wait an hour or so after you wake up. Check it before you exercise and before you drink coffee or consume anything with caffeine in it.

Caffeine temporarily increases blood pressure. Stress, fatigue, and your body temperature will also affect your reading, as will talking and moving during the reading.

WHEN IS THE BEST TIME OF THE DAY TO TAKE HIGH BLOOD PRESSURE MEDICINE? At night. Take blood pressure medication before bedtime so that it reaches its peak strength at about 6 a.m., when blood pressure rates begin to spike. **Did you know?** Blood pressure is highest between 6 a.m. and noon, the most likely time of the day for heart attacks.

WHEN IS THE BEST TIME OF DAY TO HAVE A HEART ATTACK IF YOU'RE IN A HOSPITAL? During the day. Hospital patients whose hearts stop at night are more likely to die than those who suffer cardiac arrest during the day, according to a recent study. The study doesn't say exactly why this is the case, but it suggests that care is affected by staffing issues. **Worst time of the year?** The last couple of weeks of June and the first couple of weeks of July. Many doctors say this is the time when new doctors fresh out of medical school arrive at hospitals and replace the most experienced residents, who leave to take jobs elsewhere. **Did you know?** Studies suggest a link between falling outdoor temperatures and an increase in heart attacks.

WHEN IS THE BEST TIME TO PERFORM CPR AFTER A PERSON SUFFERS A HEART ATTACK? Right after calling 911. The American Heart Association advises anyone who sees someone suffer a heart attack to first call 911 and then immediately begin pushing hard against the middle of the victim's chest as often as one hundred times a minute. The advice applies even if you're not trained in cardiopulmonary resuscitation. Experts say hands-only CPR from an untrained bystander can be as effective as CPR with mouth-to-mouth resuscitation done by someone who is certified. In fact, the heart association recommends that untrained people skip the mouth-to-mouth part. **Did you know?** CPR can more than double the survival rate for those who suffer heart attacks, because compressing the chest keeps blood flowing, but only about a third of those who suffer cardiac arrest receive CPR before emergency medical workers arrive.

WHEN IS THE BEST TIME TO CALL 911 FOR A MEDICAL EMERGENCY? This might seem obvious, but a lot of people don't know when they should call 911 rather than just have someone drive them to the hospital. Call for a suspected heart attack or stroke, a serious burn, severe pain or bleeding, a severe allergic reaction or asthma attack, or poisoning, if the person is having trouble breathing or is comatose. **The worst reasons to call?** Your cat's stuck in a tree. You want to teach your kid how to call 911. You want the police/fire department's nonemergency number. You want to make sure your new phone service works.

WHEN IS THE BEST TIME TO START COLLECTING SOCIAL SECURITY? When you turn seventy, if you think you'll live past seventy-nine. The longer you wait, the more you'll receive every month. Let's look at two examples: Mary and John are the same age, and they both will live to be ninety. They stand to collect the same amount if they retire at the same age, but Mary wants to start receiving benefits when she turns 62. She receives $19,320 a year, and by the time she dies at ninety, she has received $542,570. John waits until he's seventy to start collecting his benefits. He receives $35,340 a year, and by the time he dies, he has received $709,745. What happens if Mary dies before she's ninety? If Mary dies before her break-even age—the time at which she would have collected the same amount whether she retired at sixty-two or seventy—she would have made a wise choice. In her case, the break-even age is seventy-nine years and six months. **FYI:** If you start regretting taking Social Security early, you can do something about it, but there's a catch: After filling out Form 521, you must send the government a check that covers the benefits you've been paid—without interest. There's a chance you can come out ahead in the long run, but you should consult a financial planner or tax pro before you try this.

SOURCES

The vast majority of the answers to the questions that you've just read did not include attribution, but they are the result of an enormous amount of research. Here are the sources. In only a few cases, the author drew best-time conclusions that the sources didn't or weren't willing to make.

CHAPTER 1

Shoes—Jane Pontious, associate professor of surgery at the Temple University School of Podiatric Medicine; RealSimple.com; Terence Vanderheiden, a podiatrist in Massachusetts; Stephanie AuWerter, editor at SmartMoney.com.
Clothes—Kathryn Finney, author of *How to Be a Budget Fashionista*.

Winter coat—Kathryn Finney, author of *How to Be a Budget Fashionista*; Lisa Armstrong, "Time Is Money—Shop Smart," *Working Mother*, October 2007.

Jeans—Stephanie AuWerter, editor at SmartMoney.com.

Department store—Kathryn Finney, author of *How to Be a Budget Fashionista*.

Back-to-school supplies—Store managers and savvy shoppers.

Warehouse stores—Store managers and savvy shoppers; Michael Norton, a Harvard University marketing professor; Neal Templin, "Do Warehouse Stores Really Save You Money?" *Wall Street Journal*, September 25, 2008.

Thrift store—Thrift shop managers; Michael Gold, cofounder of TheThriftShopper.com, a national thrift-store directory.

Flea markets/garage sales—"9 Ways to Haggle Like the Pros," About.com; "Budget Decorator's Guide to Yard and Garage Sales," Pamela Cole Harris, About.com.

End an eBay auction—David Steiner, president and CEO/publisher of AuctionBytes.com.

Bid at an auction—Inchang Yang and Byungnam Kahng, mathematicians at Seoul National University, Korea, "Bidding Process in On-line Auctions and Winning Strategy: Rate Equation Approach," *Physical Review E*, June 2006; Harvard economist Alvin Roth, *American Economic Review*, 2002; Ulrike Malmendier and Young Hanh Lee, assistant professors at the University of California, Berkeley, "The Bidder's Curse," National Bureau of Economic Research working paper, December 2007.

Tickets—John Whelan, director of customer service for StubHub, *Consumer Reports*, August 2008.

Bicycles and outdoor gear—Dennis Lewon, senior editor at *Outside* magazine; Sheyna Steiner, "The Best Time to Buy . . . Anything," Bankrate.com.

Motorcycles—Dana Keeton, national sales manager of the National Motorcycle Dealers Association; American Motorcyclist Association.

Cars–Phillip Reed, consumer advice editor for Edmunds.com and coauthor of *Strategies for Smart Car Buyers* (Edmunds Publications, 2003); Sheyna Steiner, Bankrate.com.

Boats–Thom Dammrich, president of National Marine Manufacturers Association; Sheyna Steiner, "The Best Time to Buy . . . Anything," Bankrate.com.

RVs–Phil Ingrassia, vice president of communications for the Recreation Vehicle Dealers of America; Sheyna Steiner, "The Best Time to Buy . . . Anything," Bankrate.com.

Trade-in–*Consumer Reports*, December 2007.

Repair your car–Austin "The Honest Mechanic" Davis, author of What Your Mechanic Doesn't Want You to Know and the creator of TrustMyMechanic.com and MyHonest-Mechanic.com.

Get an oil change–Austin "The Honest Mechanic" Davis, author of What Your Mechanic Doesn't Want You to Know and the creator of TrustMyMechanic.com and MyHonest-Mechanic.com.

Replace your tires–*Consumer Reports*, October 2007; Mark Bilek, "Your Ride: Tires 101," *Consumer Guide Automotive*; HowStuffWorks.com.

Pump gas–National Highway Traffic Safety Administration; American Automobile Association; *Consumer Reports*, June 2008; Edmunds.com.

Consolidate home and car insurance–*Consumer Reports*, February 2007.

Cameras–Richard Doble, photography writer and the editor of Savvy-Discounts.com; Jeff Bertolucci, "When to Buy a Camera, MP3 Player, or Cell Phone," *PC World*, December 24, 2007.

Small appliances and electronics–*Consumer Reports Money Adviser*, October 2007; Carolyn Forte, homecare director for the Good Housekeeping Institute.

Replace worn electronics and appliances–*Consumer Reports*, May 2007.

TVs–Electronics store managers; Tom Merritt, executive editor for CNET, an electronics review Web site; "The Best Time to Buy Everything," *SmartMoney*, September 5, 2006.

Refrigerators and stoves–Diane Ritchey, editor of *Home Appliance* magazine; Sheyna Steiner, Bankrate.com.; Sharon Franke, kitchen appliances and technology director for Good Housekeeping Institute; *Consumer Reports*, August 2008; Jill Russell, editor, Appliance .com; *Real Simple*, October 2008.

Air conditioner–Diane Ritchey, *Home Appliance* magazine; Sheyna Steiner, Bankrate.com.

Replace your furnace–*Consumer Reports*, October 2007.

Vacuum cleaners–Diane Ritchey, *Home Appliance* magazine; Sheyna Steiner, Bankrate.com.

Computers/monitors–John Morris, CNET.com; Sheyna Steiner, Bankrate.com; Jeff Bertolucci, "When to Buy a Camera, MP3 Player, or Cell Phone," *PC World*, December 24, 2007; Canon printer spokesman Justin Joseph.

MP3 player–AbbysGuide.com; Jeff Bertolucci, "When to Buy a Camera, MP3 Player, or Cell Phone," *PC World*, December 24, 2007.

Video games–Toy Industry Association.

Toys–Reyne Rice, toy trend specialist of the Toy Industry Association; Sheyna Steiner, Bankrate.com.

Christmas tree–National Christmas Tree Association; University of Illinois Agriculture Extension Agency; Steve Nix, forester and forestry consultant for About.com.

Christmas shopping–*Consumer Reports*, December 2007.

Gift cards–Dan "Gift Card Guru" Horne, professor of marketing at Providence College; SmartMoney.com.

Holiday items–MiserlyMoms.com.

Return merchandise–Edward Fox, director of Southern Methodist University's JCPenney Center for Retail Excellence, in Dallas; Vanessa O'Connell, "Retailers Reprogram Workers in Efficiency Push," *Wall Street Journal*, September 10, 2008.

Upgrade your cell phone service–*Consumer Reports*, January 2007.

Negotiate a discount–*Consumer Reports Money Adviser*, October 2007.

Extended warranties–*Consumer Reports*, October and December 2007; *Consumer Reports Money Adviser*, October 2007; CNNMoney.com; *Consumer Reports*, May 2008.

Apply for a rebate–*Consumer Reports*, March and December 2007.

Broadway tickets–NYCTourist.com; SmartMoney.com.

Eat dinner out–Kate Krader, restaurant editor at *Food and Wine* magazine.

Grocery shopping–Teri Gault, founder of The Grocery Game, a consumer savings program; grocery store managers; Jeff Yeager, author of *The Ultimate Cheapskate's Road Map to True Riches* (Broadway Books, 2008).

Meat–MiserlyMoms.com; grocery store managers.

Eggs–*Consumer Reports*, September 2008.

Bread–MiserlyMoms.com; grocery store managers.

Fish–Numerous commercial fishermen and seafood wholesalers.

Use coupons–*Consumer Reports Money Adviser*, December 2006.

Condiments–Numerous grocers; Stretcher.com.

Turkeys–Jonni McCoy, MiserlyMoms.com; Lisa Armstrong, *Working Mother*, October 2007.

Dairy products–Jonni McCoy, MiserlyMoms.com; Lisa Armstrong, *Working Mother*, October 2007.

Frozen foods–Lisa Armstrong, *Working Mother*; National Frozen and Refrigerated Foods Association.

Fresh fruits/vegetables–U.S. Department of Agriculture; *Consumer Reports Money Adviser*, December 2006.

Farmers' market–Produce farmers; cut-flower sellers.

Bottled water–American Water Works Association; Sierra Club; Elizabeth Royte, *Bottle-mania: How Water Went on Sale and Why We Bought It* (Bloomsbury, 2008).

Champagne–Sharon Castillo, director of the Office of Champagne, USA, a trade association of growers in France's Champagne region; SmartMoney.com.

Wine–Kathleen Schumacher-Hoertkorn, CEO of New Vine Logistics, an online interstate wine retailer; SmartMoney.com.

Cookware–Hugh Rushing, executive vice president of Cookware Manufacturers Association; Sheyna Steiner, Bankrate.com.

Grills–AbbysGuide.com; Diane Ritchey, *Home Appliance* magazine; Sheyna Steiner, Bankrate.com.

Trees and shrubs–SmartMoney.com.

Tools–Hardware-store managers; home-improvement-store managers.

Lawn mowers–Mississippi State University Extension Service; *Consumer Reports*, May 2008.

Snowblowers–AbbysGuide.com.

Paint–Scruff Sermano, president of Construction Canada, an online construction directory.

Furniture–Jackie Hirschhaut, vice president of the American Home Furnishings Alliance; Sheyna Steiner, Bankrate.com.; Sharon Franke of the Good Housekeeping Research Institute.

Linens and bedding–Deb Dyer, marketing director for Cuddledown (bed and bath product manufacturer); Sheyna Steiner, Bankrate.com.

Pillows–Linda B. Ford, medical director of the Asthma and Allergy Center, Bloomingdale, Illinois.

Prom dresses–Numerous store managers.

Wedding dresses—Alan Fields, coauthor of *Bridal Bargains* (Windsor Peak Press, 2008); Stephanie AuWerter, editor at SmartMoney.com.

Weddings—Nina Callaway, event planner, About.com.

Buy jewelry—Ken Gassman, president and founder of the Jewelry Industry Research Institute; Sheyna Steiner, Bankrate.com.

Sell jewelry—Cheryl Woodland, a gemologist and appraiser; Caitlyn Kelly, "Selling Jewelry Is Mostly Pitfalls, Not Much Glitter," *New York Times,* November 24, 2007.

Gold—Michael Moore, writer on gold, gems, and diamonds; Goldprice.org.

Horses—Katherine Blocksdorf, writer and horse owner, About.com.

CHAPTER 2

Do the most difficult tasks—Norbert Myslinski, an associate professor of neuroscience at the University of Maryland.

Take a nap—Michael Smolensky, a professor of environmental physiology at the University of Texas School of Public Health at Houston and coauthor of *The Body Clock Guide to Better Health* (Holt, 2001); Richard Schwab, codirector of the University of Pennsylvania Penn Sleep Center, in Philadelphia; *Real Simple* magazine; Christine Gerbstadt, a spokeswoman for the National Dietetic Association; U.S. Department of Health and Human Services; National Institutes of Health; Mark Rosekind, researcher for NASA Ames Research Center and president and chief scientist of Alertness Solutions, a company that combats fatigue.

Play a musical instrument—Lynne Lamberg, coauthor of *The Body Clock Guide to Better Health*.

Write poetry—James Kaufman, creativity researcher and associate professor of psychology at California State University in San Bernardino, where he directs the Learning Research

Institute; Mihaly Csikszentmihalyi, author, *Flow* (Rider & Co., 2002); Harvard psychologist Howard Gardner, a leading authority on creativity; Malcolm Gladwell, "Better Late," *The New Yorker*, October 20, 2008.

Have your picture taken–*Real Simple* magazine; numerous professional photographers.

Take a landscape photograph–Great-Landscape-Photography.com; photographers.

View the moon through a telescope–Joe Rao, skywatching columnist for Space.com.

See the northern lights–Bob Swanson, *USA Today*'s assistant weather editor; NASA astronomer Sten Odenwald of the Yerkes Observatory in Wisconsin.

See the Perseid meteor shower–National Aeronautics and Space Administration.

Have a baby shower–Babycenter.com.

Ask for a date–James Sniechowski, coauthor of *The New Intimacy* (HCI, 1997); ABCNews .com; Netscape.com.

Make love–Russell G. Foster, professor of circadian neuroscience, University of Oxford; *Consumer Reports on Health,* October 2008.

Be born–Joseph Price, an economist at Brigham Young University.

Potty train–"The Best Time to Potty Train," Robyn Surdel, founder of *The Parenting Network*, a parenting blog; numerous pediatricians.

TV in a child's room–Christakis et al., "Television, Video, and Computer Game Usage in Children Under Eleven Years of Age," *The Journal of Pediatrics*, November 2004; Jean L. Wiecha, senior research scientist at Harvard School of Public Health, "When Children Eat What They Watch: Impact of TV Viewing on Dietary Intake in Youth," *The Archives of Pediatrics and Adolescent Medicine*, April 2006.

Reward/discipline your dog–Bonnie Beaver, a professor at Texas A&M's College of Veterinary Medicine and former president of the American Veterinary Medical Association; *Spirit*, Southwest Airlines' magazine, September 2008.

Walk your dog—Jean Donaldson, author of *Dogs Are From Neptune* (Lasar Multimedia Productions, 1998) and director of the San Francisco SPCA's dog-training academy; David Reinecke, founder of Los Angeles–based Dog Remedy behavioral training and exerciser of Governor Arnold Schwarzenegger's Labradors three times a week; Real Simple.com.

Sleep with pets—Mayo Clinic Sleep Disorders Center; Nikos Linardakis, author of *Ten Natural Ways to a Good Night's Sleep* (Gibbs Smith, 2007).

Adopt a pet—American Society for the Prevention of Cruelty to Animals; Adnan Qureshi, professor of neurology at the University of Minnesota.

Do a crossword puzzle—Michael Thorpy, M.D., director of the Sleep-Wake Disorders Center at Montefiore Medical Center in the Bronx.

Play video games—Lynne Lamberg, coauthor of *The Body Clock Guide to Better Health* (Holt, 2000); Netscape.com; Beth Israel Medical Center in New York City; National Institute on Media and the Family; James "Butch" Rosser, Jr., director of Advanced Medical Technology Institute and chief of the Center for Minimally Invasive Surgery at Beth Israel Medical Center.

Run—Russell G. Foster and Leon Kreitzman, *Rhythms of Life* (Yale University Press, 2005).

Lift weights—Sidney MacDonald Baker, author of *Circadian Prescription* (Perigee, 2001).

Play football—Sidney MacDonald Baker, author of *Circadian Prescription*; Roger S. Smith, Christian Guilleminault, and Bradley Efron, researchers at Stanford University Sleep Disorders Clinic, "Circadian Rhythms and Enhanced Athletic Performance in the National Football League," *Sleep*, Vol. 20, No. 5, 1997.

Swim—Thomas Reilly and colleagues at Liverpool John Moores University; Russell G. Foster and Leon Kreitzman, *Rhythms of Life*.

Clean your house–Michael Smolensky, professor of environmental physiology at the University of Texas School of Public Health in Houston and author of *The Body Clock Guide to Better Health* (Holt, 2001); "The Best Times of Day to Do Just About Anything," *Real Simple*, August 6, 2007.

Paint–*Consumer Reports*, June 2007 and June 2008.

Renovate/add on–Stephen Melman, director of economic services for the National Association of Home Builders; numerous contractors; Ed Pell, manager of market research, National Kitchen and Bath Association.

Move–American Moving and Storage Association; Jonni McCoy, *Frugal Families* (Bethany House, 2003).

Go to the post office–U.S. Postal Service.

Fill a prescription–Numerous pharmacists.

Go to the bank–Numerous bank employees; Federal Bureau of Investigation.

Go to the DMV–State motor vehicle departments throughout the nation.

Go to Social Security offices–U.S. Social Security Administration; Glenn Ruffenach, "The Baby Boomer's Guide to Social Security," *Wall Street Journal*, November 17, 2007.

Call utility companies–Numerous customer service employees.

Eat dinner–Joyce A. Walsleben, an associate professor at New York University's Sleep Disorders Center and coauthor of *A Woman's Guide to Sleep* (Three Rivers Press); "The Best Time to Eat When Losing Weight," *Prevention* magazine; *Consumer Reports' The Best of Health* (updated December 2006).

Eat spicy food–M. G. Clark, J. E. Jordan, E. Q. Colquhoun, I. M. Montgomery, and S. J. Edwards, "Spicy Meal Disturbs Sleep: An Effect of Thermoregulation?" *The International Journal of Psychophsiology*, September 1992.

Have a snack–American Dietetic Association; Netscape.com.

Drink a cup of caffeinated coffee–David Pearson, associate professor of physical education, Ball State University; National Sleep Foundation; University of Georgia; Center for Science in the Public Interest's *Nutrition Action Healthletter*, March 2008.

Drive and drink coffee–*Sleep,* December 2007; Han-Seok Seo and colleagues at Seoul National University, "Effects of Coffee Bean Aroma on the Rat Brain Stressed by Sleep Deprivation: A Selected Transcript and 2D Gel-Based Proteome Analysis," *Journal of Agricultural and Food Chemistry*, June 2008.

Defrost your freezer–Amy Dacyczyn, author of *The Tightwad Gazette II* (Villard Books, 1995).

Get a tattoo–Karen Hudson, tattoo artist and educator, About.com.

Get a haircut–Serena Chreky, co-owner of the Andre Chreky salon in Washington, D.C.; Michelle Breyer, cofounder of NaturallyCurly.com; RealSimple.com.

Throw out makeup–Faith Lawless, makeup consultant for About.com.

Trim nails–Terence Vanderheiden, a podiatrist in Massachusetts.

Take a shower–U.S. Environmental Protection Agency; Sierra Club.

Change your toilet flapper–Plumbers; National Sanitation Foundation.

Water your lawn and garden–*Consumer Reports*, May 2007; Panayoti Kelaidis, director of outreach for the Denver Botanic Gardens; Chip Tynan, horticultural-information specialist at the Missouri Botanical Garden; RealSimple.com.

Have a tree razed–Numerous tree-trimming companies.

Mulch leaves–*Consumer Reports*, October 2007.

Pick a flower–Chip Tynan, horticultural-information specialist at the Missouri Botanical Garden; RealSimple.com.

Plant grass, trees, and bushes–Connie Krochmal, BellaOnline.com's landscaping editor; Mike Reilly, owner of Reilly's Summer Seat Farm and Garden Center in Ohio Township in western Pennsylvania; Susan Banks, garden editor, "Fall Home and Garden: Best Time to Plant," *Pittsburgh Post-Gazette*, September 20, 2007.

Plant vegetables—Yardiac.com; U.S. Department of Agriculture.

Plant fruit trees—U.S. Department of Agriculture.

Kill dandelions—Ron Smith, horticulturist, North Dakota State University.

Fertilize—Ron Smith, horticulturist, North Dakota State University.

Perennials—Scott Reil, nurseryman, *The Helpful Gardener*; Gay Bechir, perennials manager at Echter's, Arvada, Colorado.

Seed a lawn—*Lawn Care for Dummies* (For Dummies/Wiley, 1998); David Beaulieu, landscape and garden writer, About.com.

Apply insect repellent—Various state and federal health agencies; WestNileVirusFacts.org; Walter Leal and Zainulabeuddin Syed, "Mosquitoes Smell and Avoid the Insect Repellent DEET," *Proceedings of the National Academy of Sciences,* August 18, 2008.

Kill wasps—Ron Smith, horticulturist, North Dakota State University; Iowa State and University of Illinois extension centers.

Dumpster dive—John Hoffman, author of *The Art and Science of Dumpster Diving* (Paladin Press, 1993).

CHAPTER 3

Fly—U.S. Department of Transportation; National Air Traffic Controllers Association; Rally Caparas, an Atlanta-based air-traffic controller and a Travelocity.com "Eye on the Sky" correspondent for CNN; Robert Baron, president of the Aviation Consulting Group, in Fort Lauderdale, Florida; numerous commercial-airline pilots; Melinda Wenner, "Why Your Flight Got Cancelled," *Popular Science,* September 17, 2008.

Buy airline tickets—Rick Seaney, CEO, FareCompare.com; American Association of Retired Persons; Anne Banas, executive editor, SmarterTravel.com.

Premium airfare—Matthew "Mr. Upgrade" Bennett, editor and publisher of FirstClassFlyer .com, a newsletter that reports on airfare-related secrets and loopholes.

Use frequent flier miles—CNNMoney.com; Matthew "Mr. Upgrade" Bennett, editor and publisher of FirstClassFlyer.com, a newsletter that reports on airfare-related secrets and loopholes.

Get bumped—Dave Pelter, CEO of Insidetrip.com, Michelle Higgins, "What to Do When Bumped from a Flight," *New York Times,* September 10, 2006; U.S. Department of Transportation.

Socialize/Jetlag—Jeremy Campbell, author of *Winston Churchill's Afternoon Nap* (Touchstone, 1998).

Vacation/winter doldrums—Dr. Matthew Edlund, director of the Center for Circadian Medicine in Sarasota, Florida, and the author of *The Body Clock Advantage* (Adams Media, 2003).

Passports—U.S. State Department.

Travel insurance—*Consumer Reports,* May 2007.

Rental car—Major rental car companies and travel agents.

Rental car upgrade—Steve Thompson, "How to Get a Free Rental Car Upgrade," *Associated Content,* March 21, 2007.

Hotel upgrade—Numerous hotel managers; Ross Klein, president of W Hotels; Daniel Edward Craig, tourism consultant, author, and former hotel executive.

Train travel—Amtrak.

Book a cruise—Travel agents; Bill Miller, author of dozens of books on ocean liners and the cruise ship industry.

Empire State Building—Tara Johnson, tour guide; Laura Bly, "Empire State Building: Stand on Top of the World," *USA Today*, October 13, 2006; *The NYC Insider* (theinsidertravel-guides.com/nyc/index.html).

Statue of Liberty—FamilyFun.com.

Niagara Falls—Numerous travel agents; FamilyFun.com.

Martha's Vineyard—Travel agents; Ann Floyd, owner of Sandcastle Realty, Edgartown, Massachusetts; Roger May, "The Need to Do Nothing," *Wall Street Journal*, September 13, 2008.

Fall foliage—Various state fall foliage Web sites.

Disney World/Land—Bob Sehlinger, coauthor of *The Unofficial Guide to Walt Disney World with Kids* (Wiley, 2007); Teresa Plowright, travel writer, About.com.

Florida Keys—EcoFloridaMag.com; Charles Passy, "At Home in the Florida Sizzle," *New York Times*, July 18, 2008.

Mount Rushmore—Rani Arbo and Greg Lauzon, "Mount Rushmore: The Four Most Famous Guys in Rock," FamilyFun.com, August 2008; *Frommer's National Parks of the American West*, second edition (Macmillan, May 2008).

Grand Canyon—FamilyFun.com; National Park Service.

Yosemite National Park—YosemiteFun.com; National Park Service.

Las Vegas—Numerous travel agents; Destination360.com.

Bermuda—*Frommer's Bermuda*, 2009.

Bahamas—The Bahamas Ministry of Tourism.

Jamaica—Jamaica Tourist Board; Michelle Higgins, "Summer in the Caribbean," *New York Times*, June 15, 2008; CheapTickets.com.

Puerto Rico—*Frommer's Puerto Rico*, 2008; EscapeToPuertoRico.com.

Cancun—Numerous travel agents and hotel concierges and managers.

Toronto–Travel agents; *Frommer's Toronto*, 2008.

Montreal–World Travel Guide, WorldTravelGuide.net; Tourisme Montréal, a group that promotes the city.

Vancouver–Vancouver Park Board; numerous travel agents.

Nova Scotia–Nova Scotia Department of Tourism, Culture, and Heritage; the Weather Channel.

London–The Londoner's Guide to London, ViewLondon.co.uk; travel agents.

Paris–Courtney Traub, journalist, editor, and Paris travel expert for About.com.

Mona Lisa–Travel agents; the Louvre.

Rome–Travel agents.

Madrid–Madrid Travel Guide, AboutMadrid.com.

Moscow/St. Petersburg–TenSquareFoot.com; Tatiana Golossovskaia Suh, who lives in Virginia but spends a month or two a year in her native St. Petersburg.

Kilimanjaro–Tom Bissell, "Up the Mountain Slowly, Very Slowly," *New York Times,* October 28, 2007.

Safari–South Africa Tourism Board; RealSimple.com; Anouk Zijlma, travel agent/editor, About.com; Zambia Tourism Board

Japan–Travel agents.

Sydney/Melbourne–Travel agents; Larry Rivera, Sydney journalist; Finn-Olaf Jones, "36 Hours in Melbourne, Australia," *New York Times,* January 6, 2008.

CHAPTER 4

Look for a job–Scott Testa, chief operating officer of Mindbridge Software in Norristown, Pennsylvania; Monster.com; Rich Gee, an executive career coach in Stamford, Connecticut; U.S. Labor Department.

Interview for a job–Michael Donovin, executive recruiter in North Carolina, author and blogger.

Ask for a raise (time)–Lynn Ellis, a career coach in Austin, Texas; Dr. Matthew Edlund, author of *The Body Clock Advantage* (Adams Media, 2003) and head of the Center for Circadian Medicine in Sarasota, Florida.

Ask for a raise (day)–Marcus Wynne, "If It's Thursday, Ask for a Raise," *Psychology Today,* September 1, 1998; John Challenger, CEO of Challenger, Gray & Christmas, an outplacement firm in Chicago; "What Is the Best Day to Ask for a Raise?" *New Mexico Business Journal,* March 2000.

Strategize, brainstorm, and solve problems–Timothy Monk, a psychiatry professor at the University of Pittsburgh's sleep and chronobiology center; Netscape.com; Tom Gegax and Phil Bolsta, authors of *The Big Book of Small Business* (Collins, 2007).

Make a presentation–Clark A. Rosen, director of the University of Pittsburgh voice center; Netscape.com.

Complain about a lazy coworker–Marcus Wynne, "If It's Thursday, Ask for a Raise," *Psychology Today*, September 1, 1998.

Disclose a disability–Brian East, lawyer for Advocacy Inc. (a disability rights group) and cochair, disability rights committee, National Employment Lawyers Association; Lana Smart, director, National Business and Disability Council; Suzanne Robitaille, "Finding the Right Way to Disclose a Disability," *Wall Street Journal,* August 26, 2008.

Start a business–Susan Ward, writer and consultant, About.com; numerous entrepreneurs.

Hold a company-wide meeting–Accountemps, a California-based temporary staffing service; Debbie Moskowitz, a psychologist at McGill University in Montreal.

Start a meeting–Morris Taylor, Illinois-based author, lecturer, and training consultant;

Tom Gegax and Phil Bolsta, authors of *The Big Book of Small Business*; Scott Snair, author of *The Complete Idiot's Guide to Motivational Leadership* (Alpha, 2007).

Drop a bombshell—James Hartley and Ivor Davies, "Note-Taking: A Critical Review," *Programmed Learning and Educational Technology and Innovations in Education and Teaching International*, Volume 15, Issue 3, August 1978.

Expect greatness—John Medina, molecular biologist and author of *Brain Rules: 12 Principles for Surviving and Thriving at Work, Home, and School* (Pear Press, 2009).

Tee off with clients—Lynne Lamberg, coauthor of *The Body Clock Guide to Better Health* (Holt, 2001); Netscape.com.

Take a vacation—Accountemps, a staffing firm; HR.Blr.com.

Bring cell phone on vacation—Dov Eden and others at Tel Aviv University presented research at the American Psychological Association's second biannual meeting in 2007 on "Work, Stress and Health."

Prepare to leave—Nancy Widmann, who wrote *I Didn't See It Coming: The Only Book You'll Ever Need to Avoid Being Blindsided in Business* (Wiley, 2007).

Quit—Lynda Donovan, co-owner of Donovan and Watkins, a Houston employment agency; Jay Jamrog, director of research for the Human Resource Institute at Eckerd College in St. Petersburg, Florida.

Counteroffer—Ken Stempson, director of human resources and administration, IntelePeer Inc., San Mateo, California; Perri Capell, "When to Take a Counteroffer from Your Employer," *Wall Street Journal*, November 6, 2007.

Fire someone—American Heart Association; Russel G. Foster and Leon Kreitzman, *Rhythms of Life* (Yale University Press, 2005); numerous managers and supervisors; John Challenger, CEO of Challenger, Gray & Christmas, an outplacement firm.

Call your financial adviser— Steve Sigmon, certified financial planner, Sigmon Wealth Management, Newport News, Virginia; Jayne Di Vincenzo, president, Lions Bridge Financial, Newport News, Virginia.

Call your accountant or lawyer—Numerous accountants and lawyers, including Mary Oder, accountant, Witt Mares, Newport News, Virginia; Michael Mulkey, attorney, Tanner & Mulkey, Newport News, Virginia.

Talk with insurance adjusters—Numerous insurance adjusters.

Call tech support—Computer manufacturers and independent support techies; Consumer Reports National Research Center.

Buy from vendors—Tom Gegax and Phil Bolsta, authors of *The Big Book of Small Business.*

Cold call—Chris Yeh, a partner at Porthos Consulting, a sales and marketing consultancy, Peterborough, Ontario, Canada; Gary Goodman, trainer and public speaker and sales, customer service, and negotiation consultant.

Cold call to big shots—Doug Fox, director of sales and marketing for Sundberg & Associates, a visual communications firm in New York City.

Send mass-market emails to moms—Maria T. Bailey, author and public speaker, *Marketing to Moms* (Prima Lifestyles, 2002).

Send business e-mails—Exact Target and EmailLabs, research firms in Indianapolis, Indiana, and Emeryville, California, respectively.

Release news—Newspaper reporters, editors, and public affairs/relations specialists.

Direct mail—U.S. Postal Service; Vertis Communications' Customer Focus Direct Mail study, September 2007.

CHAPTER 5

Make a doctor/dentist appointment—Patricia Carroll, R.N., author of *What Nurses Know and Doctors Don't Have Time to Tell You* (Perigee, 2004); Sidney MacDonald Baker, *Circadian Prescription* (Perigee, 2001)

Brush your teeth–Thomas Attin, director, Department of Operative Dentistry, Göttingen University, Germany; American Dental Association; *Consumer Reports on Health*, October 2008.

Take a pregnancy test–Office on Women's Health, U.S. Department of Health and Human Services.

Vasectomy–Several urologists.

Wean a baby–Jan Barger, lactation consultant, Wheaton, Illinois; BabyCenter.com; Michael S. Kramer et al., "Breastfeeding and Child Cognitive Development," *Archives of General Psychiatry,* May 2008

Exercise–Courtney Cunningham, owner, Zenya Yoga and Massage Studio, Newport News, Virginia.

Stretch your muscles–MayoClinic.com; Keith Cinea, senior education coordinator, National Strength and Conditioning Association; *The Cochrane Database of Systematic Reviews*; Centers for Disease Control and Prevention.

Do a cardio workout–Dr. Matthew Edlund, director, Center for Circadian Medicine, Sarasota, Florida, and author of *The Body Clock Advantage* (Adams Media, 2003); Shirley Archer, health and fitness educator, West Palm Beach, Florida; RealSimple.com.

Drink water–Gregory L. Welch, exercise physiologist, Seal Beach, California; Joey Shulman, doctor and author, Ontario, Canada; Stanley Goldfarb, a professor of medicine at the University of Pennsylvania; Lawrence Reiter et al., *From Source Water to Drinking Water* (National Academies Press, 2004).

Use sunscreen–Vincent Iannelli, a Dallas-area pediatrician, fellow of the American Academy of Pediatrics, and the author of *The Everything Father's First Year Book* (Adams Media, 2005); Environmental Working Group.

Apply ice on burns–Mayo Clinic; Yukimasa Sawada et al., "Is Prolonged and Excessive Cooling of a Scalded Wound Effective?" *Burns,* February 1997).

Chew gum–National Oral Health Information Clearing House; American Dental Association; Dr. Sanjay Purkayastha, St. Mary's Hospital, Imperial College London.

Quit nicotine gum–Tara Parker-Pope, "Obama Tries to Kick the Habit," *New York Times*, November 2, 2007.

Quit smoking–Teresa Franklin, research assistant professor of neuroscience, Department of Psychiatry, University of Pennsylvania.

Have hearing tested–Centers for Disease Control and Prevention.

Dilate eyes–William J. Vanzetta, Virginia optometrist and fellow at the American Academy of Optometry.

Have a cholesterol test–American Academy of Pediatrics.

Eat on Thanksgiving Day–Calorie Control Council; Susan B. Roberts, Senior Scientist and Director of the Energy Metabolism Laboratory, Tufts University; Tara Parker-Pope, *New York Times*; United Nation's Food and Agricultural Organization.

Have a flat stomach–Rachel A. Whitmer, investigator, Kaiser Permanente, "Central Obesity and Increased Risk of Dementia More Than Three Decades Later," *Neurology*, March 26, 2008.

Maintain weight for women–Hyun A. Park, Jung S. Lee, Lewis H. Kuller, and Jane A. Cauley, "Effects of Weight Control During the Menopausal Transition on Bone Mineral Density," *Journal of Clinical Endrocrinology and Metabolism*, October 2007.

Weigh yourself–Numerous family practice physicians.

Get a flu shot–American Lung Association; University of Michigan University Health Service; Mayo Clinic; Centers for Disease Control and Prevention; *Consumer Reports' The Best of Health* (updated December 2006).

Take an aspirin–Ramón Hermida, director of the Bioengineering and Chronobiology Laboratory, University of Vigo, Spain; American Society of Hypertension.

Take pain medication—Nancy L. Snyderman, surgical oncologist at the University of Pennsylvania and author of *Medical Myths That Can Kill You—And the 101 Truths That Will Save, Extend, and Improve Your Life* (Crown, 2008).

Take asthma medication—Jeremy Campbell, author of *Winston Churchill's Afternoon Nap* (Touchstone, 1998); Nicolaos C. Nicolaou, Angela Simpson, Lesley A. Lowe, Clare S. Murray, Ashley Woodcock, and Adnan Custovic, "Day-Care Attendance, Position in Sibship, and Early Childhood Wheezing: A Population-Based Birth Cohort Study," *Journal of Allergy and Clinical Immunology*, September 2008.

Schedule asthma appointment—Russell G. Foster and Leon Kreitzman, coauthors of *Rhythms of Life* (Yale University Press, 2005).

Treat migraines—Russell G. Foster and Leon Kreitzman, coauthors of *Rhythms of Life*.

Treat hay fever—Russell G. Foster and Leon Kreitzman, coauthors of *Rhythms of Life*; Sidney MacDonald Baker, author of *Circadian Prescription* (Perigree, 2001).

Eat fruit—Numerous nutritionists.

Eat carbohydrates/protein—Sidney MacDonald Baker, author of *Circadian Prescription*.

Eat starchy vegetables—Sidney MacDonald Baker, author of *Circadian Prescription*.

Eat vitamin-B foods—Kathleen Hall, founder of the Stress Institute in Atlanta.

Take B-1—Pharmacists; nutritionists; Krames Online, nih.kramesonline.com, a patient education resource.

Folic acid—Sidney MacDonald Baker, *Circadian Prescription*; Centers for Disease Control and Prevention.

Multivitamin—Numerous nutritionists.

Calcium and magnesium—Sidney MacDonald Baker, *Circadian Prescription*.

Zinc—Sidney MacDonald Baker, *Circadian Prescription*; the National Academy of Sciences; Arnold Palmer Hospital for Children.

Melatonin–Christopher Drake, bio-scientific staff investigator, Henry Ford Sleep Disorders and Research Center; *Consumer Reports on Health*, October 2008; National Sleep Foundation.

CHAPTER 6

Preschoolers learn–Arlene Ramasut and Theodora Papatheodorou, "Teachers' Perceptions of Children's Behavior Problems in Nursery Classes in Greece," *School Psychology International*, Vol. 15, 1994.

Older children learn–Barbara Pytel, educator and consultant, Dunn and Dunn, an education consultancy; Karol Gadwa and Shirley Griggs, "The School Dropout: Implications for Counselors," *School Counselor*, September 1985.

Start school–U.S. Department of Education; Program for International Student Assessment; International Association for the Evaluation of Educational Achievement; National Foundation for Educational Research.

Short-term memory–Keith Miller, Brian C. Syles, and David G. Wastell, "Time of Day and Retrieval from Long-Term Memory," *British Journal of Psychology*, August 1980; Jeremy Campbell, author, *Winston Churchill's Afternoon Nap* (Touchstone, 1998).

Long-term memory–Keith Miller, Brian C. Syles, and David G. Wastell; Simon Folkard, Timothy H. Monk, Rosamund Bradbury, and Joanna Rosenthal, "Time of Day Effects in School Children's Immediate and Delayed Recall of Meaningful Material," *British Journal of Psychology*, February 1977; Jeremy Campbell, *Winston Churchill's Afternoon Nap*; Michael Smolensky, a professor of environmental physiology at the University of Texas School of Public Health at Houston and author of *The Body Clock Guide to Better Health* (Holt, 2001); Harvard neurophysiologist Robert Strickgold; Joshua Foer, "Remember This," *National Geographic*, November 2007.

Learn handwriting—Steve Graham, professor of special education and literacy, Vanderbilt University; Raina Kelley, "The Writing on the Wall," *Newsweek,* November 12, 2007; Writing Instrument Manufacturers Association.

Learn a foreign language—Education Resources and Information Center Clearinghouse on Languages and Linguistics; National Network for Early Language Learning Center for Applied Linguistics; Defense Language Institute Foreign Language Center.

Learn math—Warren Esty, professor of mathematics, Montana State University.

Do homework—Numerous educators, education professors, and parents.

Take a test—Norbert Myslinski, an associate professor of neuroscience at the University of Maryland; Jeremy Campbell, author of *Winston Churchill's Afternoon Nap.*

Teach the birds and the bees—Debra W. Haffner, author of *From Diapers to Dating* (Newmarket, 2008) and *Beyond the Big Talk* (Newmarket, 2008); WebMD.com.

Teens start school day—Kenneth Dragseth, superintendent of schools in Edina, Minnesota; Mary A. Carskadon, professor of psychiatry and human behavior at Brown University and the director of sleep research at Brown-affiliated E. P. Bradley Hospital; Peter F. Flynn, superintendent of schools in Fayette County, Kentucky; American Association of School Administrators; Russell G. Foster and Leon Kreitzman, authors, *Rhythms of Life* (Yale University Press, 2005); Fred Danner and Barbara Phillips, "Adolescent Sleep, School Start Times, and Teen Motor Vehicle Crashes," *The Journal of Clinical Sleep Medicine*, December 2008.

Eat lunch—Numerous students, teachers, and administrators; U.S. Department of Agriculture's National School Lunch Program; Winnie Hu, "Busy Students Get a New Required Course: Lunch," *New York Times,* May 24, 2008; Lauren Roth, "Virginia Beach Schools Seek Waiver for Lunch Before 10 a.m.," *Virginian-Pilot*, October 9, 2006.

Try out for a sports team—Russell G. Foster and Leon Kreitzman, *Rhythms of Life*; Sidney

MacDonald Baker, *Circadian Prescription*; Dr. Matthew Edlund, author of *The Body Clock Advantage* and head of the Center for Circadian Medicine, in Sarasota, Florida.

Learn a tricky play—Charles M. Winget, Charles W. DeRoshia, and Daniel C. Holley, "Circadian Rhythms and Academic Performance," *Medicine and Science in Sports and Exercise*, October 1985; Jeremy Campbell, author of *Winston Churchill's Afternoon Nap*.

Hold a pep rally—School administrators; Jeremy Campbell, author of *Winston Churchill's Afternoon Nap*.

Surprise students—Molecular biologist John Medina, author of *Brain Rules* (Pear Press, 2009) and professor at the University of Washington's Bioengineering Department.

Visit college campuses—Joyce E. Smith, CEO of the National Association for College Admission Counseling.

Apply to colleges—Joyce E. Smith, CEO of the National Association for College Admission Counseling; Karen W. Arenson, "You're In. Can You Back Out?" *New York Times*, November 4, 2007.

Apply for financial aid—U.S. Department of Education; Joyce E. Smith, CEO of the National Association for College Admission Counseling.

Meet with a professor—Randall S. Hansen, author, public speaker, former professor, and CEO of EmpoweringSites.com.

Sell textbooks—College book store managers.

Repay student loans—U.S. Department of Education; College Board.

CHAPTER 7

Marry (month)—Numerous wedding planners.

Marry (life)—Louise Hawkley and John Cacioppo, University of Chicago psychologists, "Aging and Loneliness: Downhill Quickly?" *Current Directions in Psychological Science*,

August 2007; *American Sociological Review*; Julianne Holt-Lunstad, assistant professor of psychology at Brigham Young University, "Is There Something Unique About Marriage?" *Annals of Behavioral Medicine*, April 2008; Debra Umberson, Kristi Williams, Daniel A. Powers, Hui Liu, and Belinda Needham, "You Make Me Sick: Marital Quality and Health over the Life Course," *The Journal of Health and Social Behavior*, March 2006.

Decide to have children—Sara Schaefer Munoz, "Researchers: Have Kids Sooner if You Want a Career," *Wall Street Journal,* November 14, 2007.

Get pregnant—PregnantFocus.com; BabyHopes.com.

Give birth—Numerous doctors at hospitals and in private practice.

Stop renting—Moody's Economy.com; David Leonhardt, "As Home Prices Drop Low Enough, A Committed Renter Decides to Buy," *New York Times*, May 28, 2008.

Buy/make an offer on a house—National Association of Realtors; Gary G. Schaal, vice president of Orleans Homebuilders in suburban Philadelphia; Elizabeth Weintraub, real estate broker in Sacramento; Greg Swann, designated broker for BloodhoundRealty.com; Zillow.com.

List house for sale—Greg Swann, designated broker for BloodhoundRealty.com.

Sell a house—National Association of Realtors; LendingTree.com; Manoj Thomas, Daniel H. Simon, and Vrinda Kadiyali, "Are Precise Prices Judged to Be Lower Than Round Prices? Evidence from Market and Laboratory Data," Cornell University Johnson School Research Paper Series, 2008.

Buy flood insurance—U.S. Department of Homeland Security's Federal Emergency Management Agency.

Buy life insurance—CNNMoney.com; Independent Insurance Agents and Brokers of America.

Buy stocks—Jim Stack, president of InvesTech Research; Investopedia.com.

Start saving in a 401(k)—CNNMoney.com; Investment Company Institute; Employee Benefit Research Institute.

Cash out a 401(k)—CNNMoney.com.

Computerize your tax returns—Internal Revenue Service; Intuit, a software company; *Consumer Reports*, February 2007.

File tax forms—Internal Revenue Service; numerous accountants, including Mary Oder of Witt Mares, Newport News, Virginia.

Break bad news—Kimberly Flemke, therapist for the Council for Relationships, a Philadelphia-based nonprofit relationship-counseling group; Stephanie Watts Sussman (an assistant professor of information systems at Case Western Reserve University's School of Management), and Lee Sproull (a professor of business at New York University's Stern School of Business), "Straight Talk: Delivering Bad News Through Electronic Communication," *Information Systems Research*, June 1999.

File a lawsuit—Numerous lawyers.

Perform dangerous tasks—Sidney MacDonald Baker, author of *Circadian Prescription*; Russell G. Foster and Leon Kreitzman, *Rhythms of Life*.

Speed—Numerous police officers, sheriff's deputies, and state policemen.

Avoid traffic accidents—National Commission on Sleep Disorders Research; Russell G. Foster and Leon Kreitzman, *Rhythms of Life*; Paolo Sassone-Corsi, pharmacology professor at the University of California at Irvine; Heikki Summala and Timo Mikkola, University of Helsinki psychology professors, "Fatal Accidents Among Car and Truck Drivers: Effects of Fatigue, Age, and Alcohol Consumption," *Human Factors*, June 1994.

Drive and talk on cell phone—Donald Redelmeier and Robert Tibshirani, "Association Between Cellular-Telephone Calls and Motor Vehicle Collisions," *New England Journal* *of Medicine,* February 13, 1997; National Highway Traffic Safety Administration; John Medina, molecular biologist and author of *Brain Rules.*

Call the police–Numerous police officers, sheriff's deputies, and state policemen.

Start drinking alcohol–Doug E. King et al., "Adopting Moderate Alcohol Consumption in Middle Age: Subsequent Cardiovascular Events," *The American Journal of Medicine,* September 2008.

Drink alcohol responsibly–Sidney MacDonald Baker, author of *Circadian Prescription.*

Schedule surgery–*Consumer Reports on Health,* Fall 2007; numerous surgeons and operating-room nurses.

Seek hospital treatment–Hospital administrators, doctors, and nurses.

Get a mammogram (time of month)–Alicia Starr, medical director at Baylor University's Women's Imaging Center; American Cancer Society.

Get a mammogram (time of year)–National Cancer Institute; American Cancer Society; Brie A. Williams, Karla Lindquist, Rebecca L. Sudore, Kenneth E. Covinsky, Louise C. Walter, "Screening Mammography in Older Women," *The Archives of Internal Medicine,* March 10, 2008.

React after finding a breast lump–Various doctors and oncologists; National Cancer Institute; American Cancer Society; Russell G. Foster and Leon Kreitzman, authors of *Rhythms of Life.*

Have a Pap smear–U.S. Department of Health and Human Services; Lisa Fayed, freelance medical writer, cancer educator, and patient advocate who lives in Florida and Washington state.

Check blood pressure/medicine–Mayo Clinic; American Heart Association; Sidney MacDonald Baker, author of *Circadian Prescription.*

Have a heart attack–Mary Ann Peberdy, Joseph P. Ornato, G. Luke Larkin, R. Scott Braithwaite, T. Michael Kashner, Scott M. Carey, Peter A. Meaney, Liyi Cen, Vinay M. Nadkarni, Amy H. Praestgaard, and Robert A. Berg, "Survival from In-Hospital Cardiac Arrest During Nights and Weekends," *Journal of the American Medical Association,* February 20, 2008; World Health Organization.

Learn CPR–American Heart Association; Michael R. Sayre, Robert A. Berg, Diana M. Cave, Richard L. Page, Jerald Potts, Roger D. White, "Hands-Only (Compression-Only) Cardiopulmonary Resuscitation: A Call to Action for Bystander Response to Adults Who Experience Out-of-Hospital Sudden Cardiac Arrest: A Science Advisory for the Public from the American Heart Association Emergency Cardiovascular Care Committee," *Circulation,* April 22, 2008.

Call 911–American Heart Association; Isadore Rosenfeld, "When to Call 911," *Parade,* September 30, 2007; Rod Brouhard, paramedic and journalist, About.com.

Collect Social Security–*Consumer Reports,* October 2007.